Samuel Wheeler Pratt

The Gospel of the Holy Spirit

Samuel Wheeler Pratt

The Gospel of the Holy Spirit

ISBN/EAN: 9783743395015

Manufactured in Europe, USA, Canada, Australia, Japa

Cover: Foto ©Lupo / pixelio.de

Manufactured and distributed by brebook publishing software (www.brebook.com)

Samuel Wheeler Pratt

The Gospel of the Holy Spirit

THE GOSPEL

OF

THE HOLY SPIRIT.

The Love of the Spirit.—ROMANS xv. 30.

BY

S. W. PRATT,

AUTHOR OF "A SUMMER AT PEACH COTTAGE."

NEW YORK:
ANSON D. F. RANDOLPH & COMPANY,
38 WEST TWENTY-THIRD STREET.

TO THE

HON. CALVIN T. HULBURD,

WHO FIRST CALLED MY ATTENTION TO THE

LOVE OF THE HOLY SPIRIT,

This Book

IS AFFECTIONATELY DEDICATED.

INTRODUCTION.

THERE is a Gospel of the Holy Spirit as well as a Gospel of Jesus Christ; and neither is complete without the other.

This Gospel of the Spirit is to be found in the New Testament, and is to be read between its lines; and being unread, the Gospel of Christ is only half read. Man has a body, but is a spirit. The spirit is immortal. It is this that worships, having personal relations with the Holy Spirit. The highest thing in man is love, and the summary of the Divine character is this, "God is Love." This means that the Father is Love and the Son is Love and the Holy Spirit is Love. The fact, however, that the Holy Spirit is Love equally with the Father and the Son, and is doing a work for us which shows the same Divine Love, is little known and less appreciated by the Church.

The Father's love is revealed by what He gave; and the Son's by what He suffered; while the love of the Spirit is revealed by what He does.

We now live under the administration of the Holy Spirit, through whom the Godhead is dealing directly with the world.

This is the age of the Holy Spirit. He is the Spirit of Truth, who convicts of sin, and also renews and sanctifies the heart, making Christ's work effectual for salvation ; but for whose work all that Christ said and did would be in vain for man.

We may not only pray *for* the Holy Spirit, but pray *in* Him and *to* Him ; and He also prays with us.

Man's probation is of the Holy Spirit, and depends entirely upon His love.

He is the Divine Comforter and Helper, and as an ever-present Christ.

The communion of the Holy Spirit means all spiritual and divine blessings in one. No doctrine, therefore, can be more practical for the Church, and more profitable to know and experience, than this of the Love of the Holy Spirit ; if, indeed, this be not the department of Divine knowledge and revelation in whose unveiling lies a future development of Christian doctrine. Here, if anywhere, is the field for any new theology.

This book has been written as a devotional help for the Church at large ; to promote her spirituality, and to lead to a closer communion with the Holy Spirit.

The author would gratefully acknowledge the kindness of his beloved preceptor, the late President Mark Hopkins, who read, during the last year of his life, the outlines of this book, and to him he is indebted for words of encouragement and valuable suggestions.

"The subject," he wrote, "is one of supreme importance, and it is not apprehended as it should be, and you are right in thinking there is room and a call for a book on this subject."

He would also express his obligations to the late Prof. Ransom B. Welch, of Auburn, for reading the same manuscript, and for helpful criticisms.

Philip's "*Love of the Spirit*" has been an invaluable aid, and will be often referred to in this volume.

John Howe's rich treasury on the *Holy Spirit*, and Hare's "*Mission of the Comforter*," and other books bearing on the subject, have been carefully studied. The writer has simply undertaken to translate and re-write for this generation the work of a former one.

In an introductory note to "*The Tongue of Fire*" Dr. William M. Taylor well says: "Though we are living under the dispensation of the Spirit, it is remarkable that the work of the Holy Spirit has not received anything like the attention which it demands and deserves. Few sermons are preached upon it, few treatises are written upon it; it does not enter into the thoughts and prayers of the people of God; and in this, perhaps, more than in most things, we may find the explanation of the comparative feebleness and insufficiency of modern piety."

It is in the hope of meeting this want; of helping to open up this almost unexplored territory of the Gospel; of revealing more clearly to its readers the person, and power, and grace, and love of the Holy Spirit; of bringing them into a more intimate and loving communion with Him; and of awakening them to a more earnest co-operation with Him in the work of bringing the world to Christ, that this book is written.

CONTENTS.

CHAPTER I.

FATHER, SON, AND HOLY SPIRIT, - - - 1

The Mystery of Godliness—A Bible Doctrine—The Divinity of Christ—The Divinity of the Spirit—A Practical Doctrine—Its Truth Illustrated—The Godhead Trebly Glorified—Names and Relations—The Work of Redemption—The Spirit's Work—The Divine Glory.

CHAPTER II.

THE HOLY SPIRIT, - - - - - - 17

The Personality of the Spirit—His Holy Character—His Holy Methods—His Holy Manifestations—The Sanctifier—The Holy Comforter—The Spirit of Truth.

CHAPTER III.

THE MINISTRATION OF THE SPIRIT, - - 31

The Ministration of the Law—A New Covenant—The Law of the Spirit—The Atonement of Christ—Righteousness Apart from the Law—The Dispensation of Grace—The Spirit the Holy Executive—The Period of Redemption.

CHAPTER IV.

THE ACTS OF THE HOLY SPIRIT, - - - 44

The Spirit in the Old Testament—Christ Filled with the Spirit—Christ's Promise of the Spirit—The Acts of the Apostles—The Spirit at Pentecost—The Key to the Acts—The Spirit in Stephen—The Spirit in the Apostles—The Spirit in Paul—The Act of Regeneration—The Spirit in the Saints—The Fruits of the Spirit.

CHAPTER V.

THE LOVE OF THE SPIRIT, - - - - 60

Do you Love the Holy Spirit?—The Spirit, Divine Love—Love shown in Works—Christ's Love Rejected—Christ's Love made Efficacious—The Love of the Trinity Compared—The Condescension of the Spirit—The Patience of the Spirit.

CHAPTER VI.

THE LOVE OF THE SPIRIT IN CONVICTING OF SIN, 76

The Enmity of the Carnal Heart—The Faithfulness of the Spirit—The Righteousness of Christ—The Spirit's Love in Regeneration—Witness to Sonship—The Spirit of Truth—His Love in Defeating Satan—His Love unto Glorification.

CHAPTER VII.

THE LOVE OF THE SPIRIT IN SANCTIFICATION,   90

His Love in Regeneration and Justification—The Paraclete and Standby and Helper—His Love in Adoption—The Law of Sanctification—The Object of Suffering—His Love in Discipline—The Spirit a Deliverer.

CHAPTER VIII.

THE SPIRIT A COMFORTER, - - - - 104

Better than Christ's Presence—Kept for Jesus Christ—Afflictions and Chastisements—The Giver of Blessings—In Sickness and Death—Thy Will be Done—Complete in Christ—Helping our Infirmities.

CHAPTER IX.

THE HOLY SPIRIT IN PRAYER, - - - 119

The Gift of Gifts—The Inspirer and Teacher of Prayer—Praying for the Spirit—Praying to the Spirit—Praying in the Spirit—The Instinct of Humanity—The Philosophy of Prayer—The Spirit's Indwelling—The Duty of Prayer.

CHAPTER X.

THE INTERCESSION OF THE SPIRIT, - - 133

The Need of Intercession—Prayer and Temptation—Teaching how to Pray—Moving to Pray—Answers to Prayer—Thy Will be Done—All Prayer in One—The Intercession of Christ—Loving Faithfulness.

CHAPTER XI.

PROBATION OF THE HOLY SPIRIT, - - - 147

Blasphemy—The Sin against the Holy Spirit—Never Forgiveness—Sensitiveness to Sin—The Exceeding Sinfulness of Sin—The Privilege of Choice—The Effect of Choice—The Length of Probation—Man must *be* Saved—Dependence upon the Spirit—The Crisis of Eternity—Longer Probation Unavailing—The Spirit Grieved.

CHAPTER XII.

THE COMMUNION OF THE HOLY SPIRIT, - 164

The Apostolic Benediction—Man a Spirit—Spiritual Worship—The Law of Spiritual Life—The Cost of Redemption—Pentecost—The Love of the Spirit—Friendship and Fellowship—Prayer—Service—Growth in Grace—The Communion of Saints—Divine Fellowship.

THE
GOSPEL OF THE HOLY SPIRIT.

CHAPTER I.

FATHER, SON, AND HOLY SPIRIT.

THE doctrine of the Trinity is altogether a Bible doctrine. It stands or falls with the sacred Scriptures. Man, unaided by revelation, has believed in theism, polytheism, and atheism; but never in a Godhead of three persons.

God may be known from His works and from man His image. Further knowledge He must reveal to us. Such a revelation we have in the Bible, and this is all that it has pleased Him to give to us. Here we may expect to find the highest conception of His being and character; as full a revelation as we can comprehend, and all that we need to know for our present want. But neither now nor ever may man expect to find out the Almighty unto perfection. There shall ever be growing knowledge and fuller revelation.

"Great," says St. Paul, "is the mystery of godliness"; and the mystery shall grow even with the largest knowledge, and new mysteries shall appear. There shall be unfathomable depths and unattainable heights, and unmeasurable lengths and unexplored breadths in the Godhead.

It is conceivable that there are other modes of spiritual existence and other spiritual attributes than those we know; and that there are more wonderful revelations yet to be made. A God in whose knowledge there were no mysteries would be no God at all. The very idea of revelation implies mysteries, knowledge superhuman.

And a mystery, like a revelation, can be proved but not explained. The only question which can reasonably be raised concerning it is, Is it true? Does it stand on sufficient evidence? Its truthfulness does not depend upon the limitation of our minds. It matters not how strange or contradictory or absurd any truth may seem to be, it is to be believed, if it comes with reasonable proof. Having proved the inspiration of the Bible, it is then to be believed as the Word of God, and all of it is to be received as His word. The province of reason, after deciding upon its evidence, is to ascertain what it teaches, and to put faith in it.

A brief argument for the inspiration of the Scriptures, or the truth of their revelation, is that they stand or fall with the person and character and claims of Jesus Christ. If He be the Son of God we are to hear Him as divine authority. And He sanctions the Old Testament and gives authority to the New as written by men moved by the Holy Ghost.

The doctrine of the Trinity is found in the Bible as its revelation of the being of God, and is the grandest revelation ever made of Him, giving the highest conceptions of His being. There is, perhaps, no better brief statement of this doctrine than is found in the Westminster Catechism: "There are three persons in the Godhead, the Father, the Son, and the Holy Ghost; and these three are one God, the same in substance, and equal in power and glory."

Our present purpose is briefly to summarize the doctrine from the Scriptures and to illustrate it, with particular reference to the relation of the Holy Spirit to the other persons of the Godhead on the one hand, and to the spirit of man on the other.

In the account of the creation the name of God is plural, "Let us make man"; and elsewhere the work of creation is ascribed to the Son and to the Spirit as well as to the Father. The theophanies, or personal appearances of God, are, in the Old Testament, ascribed to the Angel of God; while, in the New Testament, it is taught that, "No man hath seen God at any time; the only begotten Son, which is in the bosom of the Father, He hath declared Him." He was God manifest, and Christ said that after His ascension the Spirit should personally reveal Him unto us. In the Psalms, Christ is called the Son of God and David's Lord; and to Him are ascribed universal authority and an eternal throne, which is referred to in the New Testament as showing His divinity. Elsewhere He is called the Messiah who should come to be Emmanuel and God manifest in the flesh. Divine titles are given to Him, and He claims to be one with the Father, and that He is in the Father and the Father in Him, and that knowing Him we know the Father. He was in the beginning with God, and God. John wrote his gospel for the very purpose of proving that "Jesus is the Christ, the Son of God." Divine perfections are ascribed to Him, such as eternity, immutability, omnipresence, omniscience, and omnipotence. Divine works are also ascribed to Him, as creation, preservation, providence, miracles, resurrection, life, and judgment. And He is worshipped by the angels; and is to receive supreme worship from all creatures, which is the especial prerogative of divinity.

The proof of the divine personality of Christ argues the same for the Holy Spirit, so far at least as to remove any presumption against it. Christ promises the Spirit to His disciples as one like Himself, who should take His place and reveal Him; through whom He and the Father would come to them; and the disciples recognized Him at Pentecost as the Spirit of promise and worshipped Him. The Spirit performs personal acts, such as knowing, searching, teaching, convicting, testifying, brooding, interceding, and loving; and executes such offices as inspiring, revealing, justifying, sanctifying, comforting, and miracle-working, being the Spirit of truth. He is given, sent, and poured out; He comes and fills and abides. Not only is creation ascribed to Him, but also regeneration, and the resurrection of the dead, and the application of grace in redemption. He may be sinned against; and the unpardonable sin is against Him, which puts special spiritual honor upon Him; and man's probation is also in His hands.

At the baptism of Christ we have heaven opened and the Holy Spirit descending upon Him, while the Father proclaims Him His beloved Son in whom He is well pleased. In His last charge, just before His ascension, Christ sums up His mission and the work of His kingdom; and, claiming all power in heaven and on earth, commands His disciples, "Go ye therefore and make disciples of all the nations, baptizing them into the name of the Father, and of the Son, and of the Holy Ghost; teaching them to observe all things whatsoever I commanded you; and lo, I am with you alway, even unto the end of the world," or " the consummation of the age."

This makes the name of the Father, and of the Son, and of the Holy Ghost alike in authority and importance; and faith in them the confession and condition of discipleship for all who hear the Gospel.

In the apostolic benediction, which prays, "The grace of our Lord Jesus Christ, and the love of God, and the communion of the Holy Ghost, be with you all," we have the same three distinct personal names and agencies of the one divine being.

At the death of Stephen, the protomartyr, "full of the Holy Ghost," looks up into heaven and sees the glory of God, and Jesus standing at the right hand of God.

The apostle Paul beseeches the Romans "for the Lord Jesus Christ's sake, and for the love of the Spirit," that they strive together with him in their prayers to God for him, making the Spirit's love an argument for prayer equal with the name of Christ.

Not to draw out these proofs at greater length, we find the divine titles, and attributes, and perfections, words and works and worship, equally and alike, given to the persons of the Father, and the Son, and the Holy Spirit in the Bible. They are made to address one another as I, thou, and he, and not as three relations or exhibitions of one person. They are thus revealed as "the same in substance, and equal in power and glory "; one God in three persons, co-equally divine, self-existent, infinite, eternal, and omnipotent, the Lord Jehovah. The Father is God, and the Son is God, and the Holy Spirit is God, and these three are one God in the glorious mystery of the divine being and Godhead. The characteristic of the first person of the Godhead is, that He is the Eternal Father; of the second, that He is the Eternal Son; and of the third, that He is the Eternal Spirit. This does not allow of posteriority, or inferiority, or subordination, except as each person has His own part in the work of redemption; but they exist in union, communion, and inhabitation.

The Father is said to give and send the Son with the sanction of the Spirit; and the Father and Son give and send the Spirit; and the Son and Spirit come to glorify the Father, and each gives Himself to us and is our God.

This revelation enlarges our idea of the divine being and glory beyond anything which otherwise could be conceived, and adds greatly to our spiritual knowledge and development and joy.

It matters not how mysterious and incomprehensible this doctrine may be, since it is taught in the Word of God, and is true as that is true.

It has, however, most important and practical

relations to man, and for this reason it was revealed to him.

The glory of man is his personality, his self-conscious, free, and responsible being.

He can know and be known, love and be loved, serve and be served, and can worship. Man has personal relations with each person of the Godhead, through whom he knows and loves and worships God, and is known and loved and blessed by God.

At first his relations were more distinctly personal with God the Father, and later with Christ the Son, and now with the Holy Spirit, so that there is no more important and practical spiritual knowledge than that which pertains to the personality of the Holy Spirit and His relations to our spirit.

This doctrine may be illustrated by analogies from nature and man, which, while they may not help us to understand the mystery, will show that it is not impossible or unreasonable, and will help us the more easily to conceive of a Trinity of persons in a unity of being.

In the formation of a mineral there are united the three forces of attraction and cohesion and chemical affinity, and, as presented to the eye, there is in the same mineral another trinity of color, shape, and size, giving the idea of body. A trinity of sides and angles is necessary to the unity of every triangle.

The sun, upon whose shining the earth depends for its light and heat, and life and growth, presents a mystery in its every ray, which is a trinity, not only of light and heat and actinism, each having its own character and effect, but may also be refracted into the seven prismatic colors. That one can see, and be warmed, and take a photograph by the same sunlight, and at the same time, is a mystery equally true and inexplicable with the Trinity of the Godhead.

Man is a trinity of spirit, soul, and body, three separate kinds of life in one, which he may so live that one may at times be almost unconscious of the others, and one may subordinate the others in a willing harmony. Within the body of man also, and necessary to its life, are eight or ten separate and interdependent and harmonious systems.

Still more mysterious is the operation within the one spirit of man of the intellect and susceptibilities and will, three distinct relations in one consciousness; and in the same man there also seems at times to be three persons—one a carnal and the other a spiritual, and a third judging between these two—a duality as well as a trinity. In the marriage union, husband and wife, twain, are one flesh, of which the man is the head; and in the family there is a still more intimate unity in the trinity of father and mother and child, the last proceeding from the other two. So also in government are the legislative, executive, and judicial functions of the one authority and power.

In the one perfect law, written by God, we find provision for the unity and development of man in the three organizations of the family and the State and the Church, inter-related and necessary to the life of man, and all centering in God.

Nor is it uncommon to find a trinity in a word, such as love, which may mean a passion, a friendship, or holy love; and there is the love of benevolence, of gratitude, and of complacency. So the word sin may mean a single sin, a habit of sin, or a sinful nature.

The being and nature of God are the foundation of religion, to know which is the highest practical wisdom for man; and since He has revealed Himself as Father and Son and Holy Spirit, whatever pertains to the relations of each of these to the other and to man is of first importance. While searching into these may be like looking into the heavens to find their infinite limit, yet by looking there have been discovered stars and suns and systems, stretching out as far as eye can pierce, and glories beyond the power of words to describe.

The development of this doctrine will yet reveal realms of knowledge and glorious relations, now only dimly seen or still undiscovered. To the writer there has seemed to be a loneliness, if not selfishness, in the divine being which is relieved and explained and made glorious by the knowledge and relations of the three persons in the Godhead.

The Godhead is thus trebly enriched for man's knowledge and love and worship; and man is trebly glorified by being in the image of the triune God. Such a divine Trinity can be possible only by a unity of nature and character and purpose; and such an One in three, and three in One, would appear to be a higher perfection of being than any other idea of being ever conceived or revealed.

The Father is holy, and the Son is holy, while the Spirit is the Holy Spirit. The Father is love, and the Son is love, and the Spirit is love, and God is love; and the same is true of the divine justice and mercy and truth. And each is personal in manifesting these attributes, and thus holds personal relations to us; so that our thought and will, and affections and consciousness, may respond to each in His operations; and while we ascribe all the manifestations of each person to God, we shall fail of personal knowledge and communion and blessing if we do not know them in their personal relations.

While each possesses all the attributes of the

others, there is in their official relations and work an exhibition of personal characteristics.

The difficulty in expressing clearly spiritual ideas and relations with words belonging to natural relations, which is great enough, is intensified when we undertake by the same words also to express divine being and relations. The names Father, Son, and Spirit are given to the persons of the Godhead because these human relations best reveal to us their personalities as manifested in the work of redemption. Fatherhood and Sonship expressed to a Jew the closest and dearest possible relationship; and in the name of the Holy Spirit as the Comforter there is also the idea of Motherhood. These words are not intended to convey to us any idea of procedure, or subordination or inequality, but only to aid us to a better understanding of the divine being and character, and especially the divine love for man. When the Father is said to so love the world as to give His only begotten Son, words are exhausted in revealing His love; and when the Father and the Son are said to give the Holy Spirit, it means that their love withheld nothing. There can be no greater revelation of the divine love. And it is in connection with the wonderful work of redemption that these relations are revealed and have practical reference to us. Thus it is that a knowledge of the persons and offices of the Father, and the Son, and the Spirit is necessary to our fullest faith and peace and blessedness. Here the mystery of godliness becomes glorious beyond expression.

In the fullness of the Divine love for a fallen and lost race the Godhead plans its redemption, wherein the Father lays upon the Son its ransom, and covenants to give Him a kingdom out of the world; and the Son offers Himself as a propitiation for their sins, to humble Himself to the human nature, and to bear the penalty of man's sin on the cross; and the Holy Spirit justifies the plan as satisfying the divine character, and also covenants to come and make effectual the sacrifice of the Son. Thus all three have a part in the covenant and work and glory of redemption, and also in the covenant and work of grace with mankind. The Father manifests His love in giving and sending the Son; the Son His love in coming and suffering, and the Spirit His love in upholding the Son and in coming and abiding.

The Father shows mercy, the Son saves, and the Spirit sanctifies. The Father plans, the Son purchases, and the Spirit completes the redemption; which shows the grace of God in its offer, the grace of the Son in its provision, and the grace of the Spirit in its effectual application.

The love of the Father in giving and the love of the Son in suffering is no greater than that of the Spirit in working, although the latter has not been magnified as it ought. Not only was the Son justified by the Spirit in the covenant of redemption, but He was prophesied and revealed in types and symbols until the fullness of time was prepared, and then was conceived of the Holy Spirit in His human nature; announced by Him as born the Christ, the Lord; anointed by Him as the Son of God at His baptism, strengthened by Him in all His sufferings, raised by Him from the dead, exalted by Him to glory; when the Spirit came to build up His church, Christ's bride, convicting the world of sin, working repentance, shedding abroad the love of Christ, speaking forgiveness, witnessing adoption, keeping for Christ until His kingdom shall have come on earth, when He will present it to Him to the glory of His grace.

Until the Son came into the world, God the Father was more manifest in the work of creation and providence; then the Son manifested God in the flesh in the work of grace as our Redeemer; and since He left the world, God the Spirit is manifest in teaching, regenerating, and sanctifying, that grace may be unto salvation; and this day of salvation is the age of the Spirit's divine administration in the world.

The Father and the Son sent the Spirit, and through His presence they come and abide with us. And the Holy Spirit is God present with us, better than the Son's brief manifestation in the flesh, gracious and glorious as that was. It was necessary that the Spirit should reveal God in Christ to the world, and personally dwell with us, working with divine power and love in and with and for us.

The Father and the Spirit glorify the Son; the Son and the Spirit glorify the Father, and the Father and the Son glorify the Spirit; and the Spirit is now glorifying the Father's law of righteousness and the Son's law of grace in love for Them and for man; not speaking of Himself, but magnifying the Son to the glory of God the Father.

The honor of one is the honor of all; the love of one, the love of all; the service of one, the service of all; and worshipping one, we worship all.

Here we get a glimpse of the glorious trinity in unity of the Father and the Son and the Holy Ghost in its nature and character and end, as manifest in the person and work of each in relation to man, and see a little into the blessedness of their presence and indwelling as we behold the co-working and harmony of the divine love where each gives His person and glory and service to the other, in the manifestation of the divine being and the bestowal of the divine blessedness.

Thus we have in the love of God, our Heavenly Father, and in the grace of our Lord Jesus Christ, our elder Brother, and in the communion of the Holy Ghost, our Comforter, a benediction of exhaustless, abiding, and eternal blessing, and would live by and die in the faith of the name of the Father and the Son and the Holy Ghost.

Well may we sing,

"Glory be to the Father, and to the Son, and to the Holy Ghost; as it was in the beginning, is now, and ever shall be; world without end. Amen."

CHAPTER II.

THE HOLY SPIRIT.

The disciples at Ephesus believed in Christ, but "had not so much as heard whether there be any Holy Ghost"; and there are many in the Church to-day who know little, if anything, of the Holy Spirit. We, who are baptized into the name of the Father, and of the Son, and of the Holy Spirit, cannot know too much of, nor too well, the persons and offices of the divine Trinity, in their being and character, and in their relations to ourselves. And, although it is true that less is said in the Bible of the Holy Spirit than of the other persons of the Godhead, for He speaks not of Himself, yet as much may be known of Him.

He it is who reveals the Father and the Son, and thereby also reveals Himself, while His works clearly and continually manifest Him.

There is no more interesting, or profitable, or practical knowledge than that which concerns the person and character and work of the Holy Spirit. If there be any person in the universe whom we need to know, with whom we ought to be well and personally acquainted, to whom we want to be devotedly attached, and with whom we want to be in constant communion, that person is the Holy Spirit.

In order to do this we must first realize that He is a Person.

Christ manifested God in the flesh so that the divine personality might be known, through the flesh, as that of any other person is known. He said: "Ye believe in God, believe also in me"; "I and my Father are one"; and "He that hath seen me hath seen the Father."

Christ is now none the less a person because ascended and glorified. Nor is the Holy Spirit any the less a person because a spirit. Man is body, soul, and spirit, but the body and soul are not the person. When the body perishes the person still lives. He acts outside of and apart from the body, and his identity is not dependent upon the body, but upon his own being. The person is the I, the ego; the being who knows and chooses and feels and wills, who reasons and uses causes, who is capable of character, having a sense of responsibility and accountability concerning right and wrong.

This personality is his spiritual being, and its exercise his spiritual life. He knows himself in his own conscious personality, which goes with him in all his actions, and is himself acting and responsible. It is the person who worships and is worshipped, of man and of God. And it is as a person, a personal spirit, that man is in the image of God. And the Holy Spirit differs not from man as a person, except that He is eternally self-existent and divine in being and attributes, which carries divine perfection into all His acts.

The Holy Spirit has intellect and will and affections. In intellect He is omniscient; in power, omnipotent; in righteousness, holy; in justice, impartial; and in benevolence, love. He is eternal and infinite and perfect in everything which characterizes spirit in its being and manifestations. He knows, teaches, guides, and strives, approves and condemns, loves and hates, and may be known, entertained, loved, and obeyed, or grieved, provoked, and rejected. We may thus commune with Him as with any other person.

As a divine person and the executor of the holy law of God, and the renewer of the heart and the applier of grace, we must have most important dealings with Him, and these will depend upon His character. His character will decide all our spiritual relations. That which distinguishes one person from another and determines what he will do personally is the character of His being, or His personal character. His character will be manifest in all He does, and will be known by what He does.

We are to believe in, and trust, and worship the Holy Spirit, because His person and words and works are divine.

That which characterizes the Godhead, but peculiarly the Holy Spirit, is holiness, for which the Spirit is named.

He is the *Holy* Spirit.

The manifestation and preservation of the divine holiness and the holy administration of the divine government are in His hands. He reveals and magnifies the Godhead in all things as holy; the Father is the holy Father, and the Son the holy Son; the law is the holy law; the Word is the holy Word; the love of God is holy love; the name of God is the holy name; the place of His manifestation is holy ground; and His dwelling-place is holy heaven. They before the throne "rest not day and night, saying, Holy, holy, holy, Lord God Almighty, which was, and is, and is to come." Even the Son of God in His work of redemption must be justified of the Spirit in the holy ransom of sinners, that He may also justify sinners who believe in Christ.

Holiness is the eternal essence of His being, and He can be only holy, and will be pleased with nothing except holiness in any part of the universe. He is the Spirit of holiness. It is His life. In creating and revealing, in regenerating and justifying, in sanctifying and ruling, in the

Law and the Gospel He is holy. He teaches, commands, promotes, delights in and blesses holiness, and abhors and condemns unholiness and destroys it forever from His presence and glory. It is ungodliness and enmity and sin. It is the Spirit who commands, "Be ye holy, for I am holy," and "follow after holiness, without which no man shall see the Lord." He will have no dealings with us except in holiness, and all His offices toward us are to make us holy and fit us for the holy presence of God. So prominent is holiness in the divine being that we call its exhibition spirituality, or the real manifestation of the spiritual life of God.

It is evident from these things that the Holy Spirit holds no second or subordinate place in the Godhead and is doing no inferior work. And man cannot know how holy God is, or what holiness is, except he be taught of the Spirit; much less can he become holy without His divine aid. No more can he know what sin is, nor how exceeding sinful it is, except the Spirit teach him; much less can he save himself from sin without the Spirit's help. Sin in man is the opposite of holiness in God, and the Holy Spirit, by His very nature, is the eternal enemy of sin and sinners. And it is as the teacher and promoter of holiness and the destroyer and punisher of sin that He works among men.

Throughout the Scriptures we see His holy methods by which He would turn and save men from sin and sanctify them unto heavenly fellowship.

First, He separated a man and then a people that they might be a holy people; and by wonderful works taught them God's being and power and providence, and ordained for them a course of instruction and discipline that they might learn His holy character and render Him holy worship.

He dwelt among them in fire and cloud, and in the holy of holies, unapproachable and most glorious. They might not come near the holy mount or touch the ark of the Lord lest they die.

Their persons and dress and food and contact and habits must be pure and clean, and their offerings and sacrifices without spot or blemish. Everything pertaining to the divine worship must be purified by water or by blood. Water and wind and fire were the emblems of purification of the heart. Places and instruments, and persons and sacrifices, were to be consecrated and sanctified to the Lord. Nothing that defileth, or worketh abomination, or maketh a lie should enter the place and presence of the Lord. Thus holiness to the Lord was impressed upon all their thoughts and worship.

The law was given most solemnly to promote

holy obedience and life. It is holy and just and good, the Spirit's standard and rule of holy living toward God and toward men, and its fearful penalty shows its holiness and the sinfulness of disobedience.

The gift and sacrifice of the holy Son of God was the least that the Holy Spirit could accept as a justification of, and penalty for, His violated law. And the life of Christ was the incarnation of divine holiness. His Sermon on the Mount declares the pure in heart blessed, for they shall see God. The appearances of the Son of God are light above the brightness of the sun, and garments white as no fuller can whiten them; and they who sit down at the marriage supper of the Lamb must have on the white robe of His righteousness.

Thus is the holiness of the Spirit manifested in spotless purity and unalloyed sanctity, in the blessing of His holy law and the wrath of its holy penalty; in holy grace in mercy; in holy pardon through the sacrifice of Christ; in holy benevolence, saving through a divine Redeemer; in holy power in regeneration, and in holy patience in the sanctification of believers. And yet none of these, nor all of them, give any adequate idea of His holiness, any more than earthly illustrations set forth God and heaven.

We can only say that holiness is the infinite

moral excellence and purity of the divine nature and character shining out as the light from the sun, and illuminating all the other divine perfections.

The Spirit of God is holy in His being, nature, and character; in all His attributes and perfections and words and works; holy in thought, feeling, will, love, and judgment; holy in person, manifestation, and companionship.

In olden time none might come into the holy of holies, where shone the glory of the divine Presence, except the high-priest with the blood of purification; but after Christ came the veil was rent, signifying an immediate approach to God by all in Christ's name. And now also in the name of Christ and because of His sacrifice, the Holy Spirit comes nearer to man than under the dispensation of law, to make known a holy righteousness apart from the law, which is by faith of Christ Jesus upon all that believe; His new law of life in Christ Jesus which frees from sin and death.

Another important manifestation of the Spirit is that of the spiritual *power* of the Godhead.

Christ commanded His disciples to tarry in Jerusalem until they should be endued with power from on high, and promised them that they should receive power when the Holy Ghost should come upon them. The Spirit had hitherto manifested His power in creation and in miracles and in gifts to men; but now greater works than these are to be done, works of spiritual grace in the hearts of men; Christ having gone to the Father and having finished His work which made the way for the Spirit's work of grace. Man must be born of the Spirit to enter the kingdom of heaven; and this work of regeneration is not possible by any other might or power, or by the will of the flesh, but only by the Spirit of God. Christ taught this to Nicodemus as a prime truth, a first necessity. Spirit must be born of Spirit. The provision which Christ made for redemption was all vain unless the Spirit made it efficacious through His regenerating work.

For its further existence and growth the Church is now dependent upon the power of the Spirit, through His personal work with its members and in the world. And this power, which is so manifest in regeneration, He will also manifest in the work of sanctification until He shall present the Church to Christ, holy and without blemish.

The methods of the Spirit's work are likened unto the action of water and wind and fire, the great purifying elements of nature. He may come like the gentle shower, the running brook, the great river, or the ocean-tide in His cleansing power, and like the mountain torrent, or the overwhelming flood, or the tidal-wave in His holy wrath. Sweetness and purity follow and everything is refreshed and renewed.

At Pentecost His coming was as the rushing, mighty wind, which purifies and also vivifies. We know not whence it cometh nor whither it goeth, but its effects are manifest. So is the work of the Spirit. Now He whispers as the gentle breeze, as a still small voice, so that one scarcely recognizes His presence; again He comes as the tempest and hurricane and cyclone, when nothing can withstand Him. The place is shaken with His presence, and strong men bow before Him; again His power sweeps over the country like a storm-wave of spiritual influence from the mountains to the sea. The power of His coming at Pentecost was also like fire, which can warm and bless with heat and light, or beginning in a match devastate and devour a forest or prairie, or city in its blackening course. This is also the great purifier by which the gold is refined from the dross, or the germs of contagion and plague are destroyed.

So does His holy power bless the righteous and punish the wicked, separating righteousness and sin. The prophet saw the blessed time in the latter days, when God would pour out of His Spirit upon all flesh, and it should come to pass that whosoever should call on the name of the Lord should be saved. This outpouring characterizes the era of salvation.

And the same holy power which works like the wind and water and fire comes also like a dove, as when He descended upon Christ at His baptism and annunciation, the Spirit of gentleness and peace, of brooding mother-love and help, full of sympathy and kindness, benevolent and beneficent.

The Spirit of the Lord was upon Jesus Christ and filled and sustained Him, and He in all His words and works and ways manifested the Spirit's character and work, and never man spoke or acted or loved like Christ, whose gentleness made Him greater than king or hero or conqueror.

Again, the Spirit is called the Comforter or Paraclete, the Advocate, the Standby and Helper, who should take Christ's place and be to all the Church what He was to His disciples, present always with divine power to heal and help and comfort and save, by whom the Father and the Son would come to us and dwell in us, bestowing the peace of God.

As the Comforter He is very near and dear to the ignorant and erring and weak and faint and troubled disciples. Nor does He afflict willingly, but as a friend, wise and good, who knows how to comfort those in affliction with the comfort of God.

In this connection He is called the Spirit of Truth. He is the revealer and teacher of truth.

And truth is only another name for the divine character and will in their unchangeableness, which is the basis of faith. His word is truth, and whether in law or prophecy, or Psalm or Gospel, is holy. And in precept and command and promise the Spirit verifies and sanctions it with sure rewards and penalties, magnifying His truth, above all His name.

And Christ is *the* Truth which is the power of the Spirit unto salvation, which He most delights to teach and verify. Christ is the one divine fact and reality and verity, so great that there is nothing else to be believed or known by the sinner, since to know Him is life eternal. He said of the Spirit: " He shall teach you all things, and bring all things to your remembrance whatsoever I have said unto you "; " He will guide you into all truth "; " He shall take of mine and shall declare it unto you."

Again, and this shows what truth the world needs above all else : " And He, when He is come, will convict the world in respect of sin and of righteousness and of judgment ; of sin, because they believe not on me ; of righteousness, because I go to the Father and ye behold me no more : of judgment, because the prince of this world hath been judged."

He does not say smooth things and deceive or leave in sin to perish ; but reproves and convicts that He may bring to repentance, and also that He may show the righteousness of Christ without the law, and give peace to those who believe in Him. His comfort is true and abiding, helpful and saving unto eternal life to believers, upon whom He bestows His regenerating power and grace. He convicts of sin that sinners may know their sin and their need of Christ, and embrace Him. And the greatest sin of all in the eyes of the Spirit is their unbelief in Christ, when His death shows the exceeding sinfulness of their sin and their condemnation of God, in that the Son of God must die that the Spirit might come to them or do aught for them, so that every gracious manifestation of His holy power and grace is through Christ.

The Spirit's comfort is all in Christ, and while He can do nothing except in His name, He can wash and justify and sanctify in His name an idolater or blasphemer or drunkard, even the chief of sinners, making him a new creature in Christ Jesus. And this same holy power which is manifest in regenerating, quickening from death in sin, will also keep alive and strengthen and sanctify until the sinner shall be made complete in Christ, and be presented in His name without reproof and blameless and with exceeding joy, in the great day, saved evermore. By the power with which He delivered Jesus from

Satan and raised Him from the dead, will He deliver His saints and raise them up with Him. Freed from sin, the death of the body shall not separate them from Christ, but rather bring them to His presence to behold and partake of His glory.

The power of the Holy Spirit in promoting holiness is like Christ full of grace and truth. To Him are committed all the benefits and blessings of the Father's love and the Son's sacrifice, so that as the promise of the Father and the gift of the Son without measure, He is indeed the Holy Spirit of Truth and the Comforter. Nothing shall separate us from the love and power of the Holy Spirit, which is in Jesus Christ our Lord. Whom He has justified and sealed as Christ's He will also sanctify and glorify.

Seeing, therefore, that all things of Christ and salvation are in the hands of the Holy Spirit, and that we now live under His divine administration, shall we not prize it, as the best and greatest of all our privileges and blessings, to have the personal acquaintance and friendship and love and communion of the Holy Spirit?

CHAPTER III.

THE MINISTRATION OF THE SPIRIT.

THERE are revealed in the Bible glimpses of the administration of the divine government, in the fall of the angels who left their first estate and were reserved in everlasting chains under darkness unto judgment; in the covenant of redemption; in the councils of eternity; in the creation of the world; in the fall of man; in the incarnation of Christ; in the judgment of the great day and in the final glory of heaven.

The period of creation ended and that of redemption began when God rested from His labors; and ours is the day of salvation, the age of redemption, which shall continue until the consummation of the age in the glory of the general judgment.

God's ministration in nature was to the glory of the divine power and wisdom and goodness, but the ministration of redemption excels in the supreme glory of the divine grace. So far as we know, this is the crowning glory of the ages and kingdoms of God's eternity, and the last and highest revelation of His being; yet there may be divine attributes to be revealed which shall shine brighter even than mercy, glories which excel.

In the divine administration of human affairs there are two periods—the ministration of the law and the ministration of the Spirit; the law represented by Moses, and the Spirit by grace and truth which came by Jesus Christ, called sometimes the Old and New Testaments or covenants, or the Law and the Gospel.

The ministration of the law, which was of death, written and graven on stones, had such glory that the children of Israel could not look on the face of Moses for the splendor of his countenance; but this was not abiding. So did the majesty of God appear when He gave the commandments with awful solemnity and sanctions of life and death, that Sinai flamed and smoked and quaked and thundered, and the people dared not come near nor touch it lest they should die. The law revealed the holiness of the divine being and character and gave heaven's standard of eternal righteousness, and set forth the rule of man's perfection. Well is Moses called the greatest lawgiver of the old world. This was the perfect law of God, benevolent and beneficent in its end and work, the law of spiritual order and beauty and peace and blessing. As universal ruin and chaos would follow the overthrow of the divine authority through natural laws, so would spiritual death follow disobedience to His laws written on stone and in the heart of man.

The glory of government, divine and human, is in good laws and in their faithful execution. Upon this, in large measure, depend the welfare and happiness of the governed.

And this law given by Moses is as good as it is holy and just. It blesses the obedient unspeakably, and restrains and punishes only the evil. The second table would give us perfect homes and all personal rights, securing life, chastity, property, reputation, and good-will, and promoting temperance, virtue, honesty, truthfulness, and brotherly love. And toward God the first table provides for knowledge, reverence, worship, and supreme love and choice and service, forbidding atheism, idolatry, and profanity. Under such a law and for such a glory was man created—the law and glory of heaven as well as of earth.

It is evident that any change in the law, or any failure in its execution, would be dishonorable to God and injurious to man. No penalty could be too severe for disobedience when its reward was life eternal. The welfare of the universe turns upon its supreme authority and unchangeableness. The glory of its justice is as great as that of its holiness and goodness; and this shall be manifest in the great day alongside the glory of redemption. This law is called the ministration of death, because it reveals and condemns sin, whose work and wages are death. It remains, however, always and everywhere the holy law of God, and its glory shall never be taken away. Under it sinless man would attain perfect blessedness in the glory of the divine presence forever.

And under the ministration of the Spirit there is not a whit abated of its holiness and condemnation of sin; but rather is the law magnified and made more glorious in its everlasting righteousness.

But how shall the Holy Spirit with this His law, whose glory must never be tarnished, minister anything but death to the disobedient? And under its covenant of works no man can be saved.

Not interfering with this covenant, not abrogating one letter of the law, but honoring it, a new covenant has been made without the law; yet in the very spirit of the law.

In the counsels of the Godhead, born of the love of the triune God, the covenant of redemption was made; planned by the Father, procured by the Son, and ratified by the Holy Spirit, in which, because of the love of the Father, the sacrifice of the Son, and the work of the Spirit, the covenant of grace—a new and still more glorious covenant than that of works under the law, and yet in harmony with that—was offered to man. And this covenant or dispensation of grace was to be under the special administration of the Holy Spirit.

Attention, however, is given both to the Spirit's work in administering redemption and to the work of Christ in providing it, when it is called the dispensation of the Gospel of Christ.

In the Levitical law and in the Prophets the Spirit foretells, in what might be called His dispensation of prophecy, the glory of the coming of Christ, and the greater blessings of the dispensation of grace. The sacrifices foreshadowed the Lamb of God, who should take away the sins of the world. Its rituals told of cleansing and forgiveness and reconciliation. The Son of God must be made in the likeness of sinful flesh; made under the law and fulfil its righteousness; upon Him were laid the sins of the world, and He should suffer their penalty: pouring out His soul unto death, the substitute and sacrifice and ransom for guilty man. It pleased the Lord to bruise Him, and the Spirit of the Lord was upon Him: filling Him and sustaining Him in His mission, to which He publicly anointed Him. The righteousness of the law was fulfilled in Christ and He became the end of the law for righteousness to every one that believeth. God was just, and the justifier of him who believed in Christ.

The ministration of death had its satisfaction in the sacrifice of Christ, by which believers were freed from the law of sin and death.

The proclamation of the Spirit by Isaiah of the new covenant, even the sure mercies of David, was now made to the world. For three short years the Son of God fulfilled His divine mission, walking, talking, and living among men, revealing more clearly the kingdom of heaven and laying the foundation of the Christian Church. During this time, He to whom was given the heathen for an inheritance, and the uttermost parts of the earth for a possession, administered on His footstool His own rightful and purchased kingdom.

But He, the Prince Royal of the kingdom of Heaven, in whom at last every knee shall bow and every tongue confess to the glory of God the Father, was a man of sorrows and a servant in His own dominion; whose own received Him not, but denied and rejected Him and put Him to death; knowing not that He should draw all men unto Him, when lifted up, as between heaven and earth, Lord over both. Now was come the long-prophesied fullness of time, when Christ was personally present with His Church.

No wonder the disciples would not allow the thought that He should go away, and could not take in the meaning of His death. What could be more glorious than His presence and work!

It seemed as if all would be lost and the kingdom of heaven would come to an inglorious end.

But He says to His disciples, "It is expedient for you that I go away." There was yet to come the glory that excelleth. Again He says, as He died, "I have finished the work which the Father gave me to do." Until this was done, the Comforter, the greatest gift of the Father and of the Son to the Church, and whose ministration should bring in the final glory, could not come unto us.

He who discerned spiritual things and whose was the power of God, should abide with us forever and show unto us the things of Christ; glorifying Him as He was not glorified when on earth. Without the Spirit's coming and work all that Christ did would be vain, and the kingdoms of this earth would not become the kingdoms of our Lord and His Christ. The Spirit should manifest the glory of God in the salvation of the Church of Christ and be even more to it and nearer than a present Christ.

Old John Owen, whose writings concerning the Holy Spirit are a rich treasure, says:*
"When God designed the great and glorious work of recovering fallen man, and the saving of sinners to the praise of the glory of His grace, He appointed in His infinite wisdom two great means thereof. The one was the giving of His

---
* Owen on the Holy Spirit, Book I., chap. i.

Son for them; and the other the giving of His Spirit unto them. And hereby way was made for the manifestation of the whole blessed Trinity, which is the utmost end of all the works of God. Hereby were the love, grace, and wisdom of the Father, in the design and projection of the whole; the love, grace, and condescension of the Son, in the execution, purchase, and procurement of grace and salvation for sinners; with the love, grace, and power of the Holy Spirit, in the effectual application of all unto the souls of men, made gloriously conspicuous." "But when once that first work was fully accomplished, when the Son of God came and had destroyed the works of the devil, the principal remaining promise of the New Testament, the spring of all the rest, concerned the sending of the Holy Spirit unto the accomplishment of His part of the great work which God had designed. Hence the doctrine concerning His person, His works, and His grace is the peculiar and principal subject of the New Testament, and a most immediate object of the faith of them that do believe."

Christ laid the foundations of the Church, and the Holy Spirit builds thereon the glorious temple until the top-stone thereof shall be laid with shoutings of "grace, grace unto it." The Holy Spirit's presence more than makes up the absence of Christ, and is God manifesting Himself to us in the place of a present Christ. He is the operative and efficient source of all spiritual good. The Church must have His presence and be endued with His power for her work.

The Spirit and the Word of God go together as the hand and the sword, the hand giving power to the sword. The Father and the Son send the Spirit, who is the present and all-powerful teacher and sanctifier and comforter of the Church.

We cannot have too exalted a conception of the gift of the Spirit's divine, personal presence, who has all knowledge and wisdom and power and grace and love in the application, and perfection and sealing of the grace of God in redemption; nor can we feel too deeply our dependence upon and need of Him in all His offices; nor shall we get the full measure of His blessing if we fail to see in all His operations the work of His own personal, free, and sovereign will.

And while He does not speak of Himself, but works in the name of Christ, yet He works with His own divine power and manifests His own grace and glory.

While Christ is the author and finisher of that which makes faith possible, and upon which it rests for salvation, the Holy Spirit is the author and finisher of our participation in and union with Christ by faith. So dependent are we on

Him that no man can say that Jesus is the Christ but by the Spirit of God.

Thus it appears that, since the coming of Christ and His death, and because of these, the administration of the divine sovereignty has been in the hands of the Holy Spirit, as the executive officer of the Godhead; so that we now live under the administration of the Holy Spirit, and have to do with Him immediately and practically in all our relations to God; and are dependent upon His illumination and power and grace for our knowledge and help and hope. This, the Christian dispensation, and the golden age of the Church, and the glory of the ages, is the period of the administration of the Holy Spirit, through whose divine offices we are brought out from the bondage of death into the glorious liberty of the sons of God.

This phase of the divine government finds illustration and parallel in human governments which are also ordained of God. While a government is one and in all departments equally sovereign, it naturally divides into the legislative and executive and judicial departments, each of which exists for the other and supplements the other, all necessary to sovereignty.

In the kingdom and sovereignty of God, the divine Father is the head of authority, the Law-giver; the divine Son is the Judge, to whom is given the salvation and judgment of this world; and the divine Spirit is the Executive, administering the Law and the Gospel and building the kingdom of Christ.

When Christ left the heavenly glory, and took upon Him the nature of man, and became obedient unto the death of the cross, He came not to rule, but to mediate peace.

The executive efficiency, the personally present power, must needs be the divine Spirit, who knows the mind of God, being Himself divine; and so is at one in His administration with the divine being and character and will; and who as a Spirit knows also immediately the spirit of man, before whom it is transparent.

By His divine and human nature Christ could sympathize with man and mediate with the Father. Being a Spirit, and coming immediately into His very consciousness, into personal contact with His mind and will and sensibilities and conscience; illuminating, convicting, actuating, regenerating; working repentance and faith and all graces, the Holy Spirit, as none other, can reveal and teach and work the works of God directly in man. He by His omnipresence could come nearer to each one and to all the world than could God manifest in the flesh, so that the administration of the personally present

Spirit meets exactly and fully all the wants of the universal Church.

Christ was with us in the body and limited by the body; the Holy Spirit is with us and in us, always and everywhere abiding and ministering.

Coleridge brings out these relations of the Godhead as "the I Am empowering, the Word informing, and the Spirit actuating."*

Spurgeon says: "Christ is the medicine and the Spirit is the physician."

The work of the Father and the Son is completed, so far as the Law and the Word are concerned, except judgment, and nothing more is to be added to the revelation of righteousness or grace.

The executive acts under the constitution of the government and according to the decrees of the legislative and judicial departments, conducting the sovereignty for the glory of the sovereign and the good of the subjects. The character of the administration of the Holy Spirit is already determined by His own holiness, and by the law and the Gospel its limits are defined. He is the Holy Spirit and the Spirit of truth. Whatever is the Father's will and the will of the Son is the will and the work of the Spirit. Whatever is

---

* "Moral and Religious Aphorisms," vi.

anti-Christ is anti-Spirit, for He works only in Christ's name and for His glory. Man is now dealing directly with the Spirit of God, and comes to God through Him, and is dependent on Him for light and strength and grace.

To sin against the Holy Ghost is worse than idolatry of old; is to drive Him out of one's heart and make the body a temple of mammon. To neglect, to despise, to grieve, to reject Him, is to bring upon us the displeasure of the Godhead. And nothing so offends the Holy Spirit as disbelief and neglect and rejection of Christ, except to call Him, the Holy Spirit, unclean and His work that of the evil one, which hath never forgiveness.

The glory of God, the redemption of Christ, and all the affairs of His Church are now in the hands of the Holy Spirit, whose administration is the most glorious period of the divine sovereignty, in the ministration of the covenant of grace; and to live in this age and under His administration is the most blessed privilege man has enjoyed. And when this period shall be finished and the work and day of redemption shall be ended, then the Spirit shall gather up and commit all things of this world to Christ, when He shall come with the glory of the Father and the holy angels to judge the world, when all shall confess in the name of Christ that He is Lord to the glory of God the Father.

CHAPTER IV.

THE ACTS OF THE HOLY SPIRIT.

LIVING as we do under the dispensation of the Holy Spirit, having to deal with Him directly and immediately in all our divine relations, and dependent upon Him for instruction and strength and grace, it becomes an object of first and deepest importance to know His character and will and acts. The constitution of the government and the platform of the dominant party will set forth, in general, the character of an administration; yet we await with solicitude the President's inaugural and the selection of his Cabinet and the exercise of his official authority, to learn in particular what will be the policy of an executive.

In general, the Spirit of God has all divine attributes and perfections, but He is particularly the Holy Spirit, working with divine power in personal relations with men. He is also known by His Law, which gives the great principles of righteousness and their practical application to the affairs of life. The Gospel further sets forth His new law of grace in Jesus Christ. Then comes the practical development of these principles of righteousness and grace in His personal administration and upbuilding of the Church of Christ.

In the days of Noah the Spirit of God strove with that generation, and in vain, until there was no other alternative except their destruction. He was promised unto the house of Israel to be poured out on them; and, looking forward to His administration in the last days, the days of salvation, the prophets foretell that the Spirit of God shall be poured out on all flesh, and they shall prophesy and see signs and do wonders, and whosoever shall call on the name of the Lord shall be saved. It is especially foretold of the Christ that the Spirit of the Lord shall rest upon Him, and this shall be the moving of His wonderful works.

In connection with His incarnation the parents of John the Baptist, His forerunner, and Mary, His mother, were full of the Holy Spirit, who also came upon the aged Simeon, and John himself was also full of the Spirit from his birth. Christ was baptized with the Spirit and announced by Him as the Son of God, and filled with His presence and power. So He endured the temptation in the wilderness and went forth upon His mission until He was offered up of the Spirit for the salvation of the Church. Thus anointed, filled with and strengthened by the Spirit, whatever Christ manifested of the Godhead, and said and did, was also moved by, and sanctioned and done by, the Holy Spirit. The Life of Christ was the manifestation in the flesh of the personal character of the Spirit, as also were His words and work. He was God with us showing what God the Spirit would be and do in us and with us and for us; when He should complete in His administration what was begun by Christ, doing all in His name.

When Christ sent forth His disciples He promised them the presence of the Spirit, who should speak through them, and guide and protect them. And just before His death He revealed the Spirit's coming as the special promise of the Father, whose spiritual presence should be better than His own bodily presence; who should be the Comforter of the Church, teaching them all things, and especially the things of Himself, and glorifying Him; and thus it was that He would be with them always, even unto the end of the world. They could do nothing without the Spirit, and should tarry in Jerusalem until they were endued with His power from on high. So in prayer they awaited the baptism of the Holy Spirit. It was His coming upon them that made them efficient witnesses of the Word of God, and enabled them to do the work of Christ. And the truth of the common-law maxim holds good here as in other cases, that what one does through another he does himself, making their words and works also those of the Holy Spirit.

The book of the Acts of the Apostles would better be called the Acts of the Holy Spirit. It really concerns but two of the apostles; and ends its account of the Acts of the Spirit by Peter, where those of Paul began; and gives of their Acts only those which pertain to the Acts of the Spirit through them in laying the foundation of the Christian Church and in preparing the way for its spread among the Gentiles, or its universality. As soon as Paul reaches Rome and has fulfilled his mission as the Apostle to the Gentiles the book closes.

The first things of a government, or church or other institutions, are most important in determining their character and the law and life of their development. For this reason we give great reverence to the fathers who laid the foundations of our government and consult their writings in the interpretation of its constitution. In the Acts of the Apostles we have the first things, the precedents, for the constitution and life and work of the Church.

Here we are to look for its organization and government and spirit. As the life of Christ is our example for living, so the work of the Spirit is our example for working. Further revelation of divine truth was to be in words and in acts.

The day of Pentecost was the beginning of the dispensation of the Spirit, the inaugural day of His work, the era-marking day of the Church of Christ. Here we have the firstfruits of the Spirit, a sample of what He will always do, and an earnest and pledge of the continuance of His whole work until its consummation in glory. There is little danger of our making too much of this day, or of resting too strongly upon its promise.

Preparation was ended; Christ had gone to His Father, and greater works are to be done than the Church had hitherto seen. The Holy Spirit now shows forth His policy practically by His work, and His methods of work by working, and His application of grace by ordaining means of grace.

The constitution of Christ's kingdom has been established unchangeably, and now we are to have its development. Doctrine is to be made duty, and principle to become practice and spirit life. On this day the Spirit was poured out with a fullness and power and presence never before known. His coming was as a rushing mighty wind, and like as a fire which sat upon each of them, the symbols of spiritual presence and power. "And they were all filled with the Holy Spirit, and began to speak as the Spirit gave them utterance."

In these words, "filled with the Holy Spirit,"— repeated nearly a score of times in the Acts, words which cannot be magnified too highly by the Church,—we find the key to the whole book. He filled the apostles and disciples so that they did His acts, working through His power and gifts.

His first gift to them and work through them was *utterance*. So wonderful was this that it amazed all who heard them. Peter, filled with the Spirit, had a new understanding of the things of Christ; and with all boldness began to preach Jesus the Christ, as prophesied in the Scriptures, and as manifested in His life and death and resurrection; and that this which they now saw of the work of the Spirit was the promise of the Father and of Christ; and the effect of his preaching was that men were pricked in their hearts and brought to repentance and received of the gift of the Spirit, and three thousand were added to the Church.

Again, after working miracles and wonders and praying, the place where they were assembled was shaken, and they were all filled with the Holy Spirit, and witnessed of Christ with great power; and great grace was upon them, and a spirit of self-denial and love for the poor was wrought in them.

Ananias and Sapphira in trying to deceive the apostles were charged with lying to the Holy Spirit and with tempting the Spirit of the Lord, and were smitten with death as an example to all time to come of the solemnity of dealing with the Holy Spirit and of His jealousy for the honor of the Church of Christ. Peter preaches again that God had exalted Christ to give repentance and remission of sins, and that the Holy Spirit is witness with them of these things.

Stephen is a marked example of one full of the Holy Spirit and power; who wrought wonders among the people and preached Christ with all boldness; whose very face shone with His indwelling as the face of an angel; who went to martyrdom as to triumph, seeing the heavens opened and the glory of God and Jesus Christ standing on the right hand of God; and who, committing his spirit to the Lord Jesus, fell asleep. Full of the Spirit, Stephen lived blamelessly, preached boldly, trusted joyfully in Christ, suffered patiently, forgave freely, and died triumphantly.

We find Peter and John laying their hands on the people and imparting the gift of the Holy Spirit. Philip, one of the deacons, was also filled with the Holy Spirit and directed in his work, and, in one marked instance, was sent toward Gaza, there to meet the Ethiopian eunuch, and, having instructed and baptized him, was caught away. One of the most celebrated instances of His power and work—a sample, not of what He usually does, but of what He can do, that the Church may not despair of any—was the conversion of Saul of Tarsus, whom He met on his persecuting tour, and brought to see that he was persecuting the Christ, and to acknowledge Him as the Lord. And to him also He sent Ananias, who was told that he should find Paul a praying disciple.

Paul was also filled with the Holy Spirit and began at once to preach Christ, and went forth as the apostle to the Gentiles. The Spirit at this time prepared Peter by a vision to go to Cornelius, a Gentile, and to show Christ to him, and then fell on them all alike, that they might know that "to the Gentiles God had granted repentance unto life." Barnabas, who was full of the Holy Spirit and faith, went forth to preach, and much people were added to the Lord. The Spirit also watched over imprisoned Peter, and delivered him to his praying brethren.

At His command and under His direction Paul went forth on his mission to the Gentiles, and His disciples were filled with joy and with the Holy Spirit; and the special proof of his ministry was that the Holy Spirit was given to the Gentiles. At one time the Spirit forbade his going to Asia, nor suffered him to go to Bythinia, but sent him over to heed the voice from Macedonia to a Roman colony, to begin the conquest of the Latin races for Christ.

The ministers whom Paul set apart were made overseers by the Holy Spirit to feed the Church of Christ. Throughout his three great missionary tours the Spirit guided and sustained and filled him with wisdom and grace and power, and then prophesied his imprisonment and his journey to Rome, where he gave favor and power to his preaching until the Church was established in the centre of the world, and the way was prepared for its spread over all the earth. The secret of Paul's glorious ministry—the hiding of his power —was that he was filled with the Holy Spirit, who was building up through him the Church of Christ.

Thus are we warranted in claiming that the Acts of the Apostles are the acts of the Holy Spirit, and intended to teach the character and methods of His administration of the kingdom of God on earth. He took of the things of Christ and showed them unto His disciples, and gave them understanding and utterance and wisdom and strength; so filling them that they preached with such power over men's consciences that they trembled and repented, and great grace was upon them, so that they were enabled to endure trials and afflictions with joy for Christ's sake; and by them the Church was spread abroad over Asia and Macedonia and Greece, and even to Rome and Ethiopia.

THE ACTS OF THE HOLY SPIRIT. 53

With these acts of the Holy Spirit before us, we shall not hesitate to receive the further testimony of the apostles concerning His teaching and work. The words of those so filled with the Holy Spirit and doing His works must be true, and the words of inspiration. And this they claim that, as in the Scriptures of the Old Testament, "Holy men of God spake as they were moved by the Holy Spirit"; so they were chosen and set apart to bear witness to Christ and His resurrection; and their words were not the words of men, but in truth the words of God. This truth of His inspiration He makes still plainer by His illumination of it, showing His mind in it and bringing to light the deep things of God; and thus, by enlightening the understanding of the reader, applying it to the heart and conscience; searching even to the dividing of soul and spirit and discerning the thoughts and intents of the heart; making it piercing as a sharp two-edged sword, He convicts of sin and of righteousness and of judgment as Christ foretold of Him. He is the wisdom and the power behind the word and preaching of Christ; and in all the work of the Church He wields the sword, the Word of God, and makes all means of grace effectual to their appointed ends. In that greatest spiritual work, wherein a sinner is renewed in the spirit of his mind, and becomes a new creature in Christ Jesus, enabled to repent and embrace Him by faith, he is born of the Spirit. He enters the kingdom of God only through the washing of regeneration and renewing of the Holy Spirit. The cleansing of the heart, the speaking of pardon and peace, the spreading abroad of the love of Christ, the witness of adoption, are all His blessed work. The whole change from the carnal to the spiritual, whereby idolaters, drunkards, the worst of men and the chief of sinners, are washed and sanctified and justified, is in the name of the Lord Jesus and by the Spirit of God. And so are they changed, who were walking in the lusts of the flesh, that they live in the Spirit and bring forth His fruits of love, joy, peace, long-suffering, gentleness, goodness, faith, meekness, and temperance, and walk in all goodness and righteousness and truth.

In His work of sanctification He keeps from the love of sin, delivers from temptation, and works all righteousness; sustains in trials, disciplines in holiness, guards from the evil one, makes to grow in grace, teaches to pray, gives His fellowship, fills with love and joy and hope of glory, seals unto the day of redemption, when He presents those whom He has justified in Christ faultless and blameless before Him with exceeding joy.

Thus the help of the impenitent and the hope

of the renewed are alike and always in the work of the Spirit, beginning and ending their salvation through Christ. Here in the power and grace and love of the Spirit we have the assurance of the perseverance of the saints. And the same power of the Spirit which raised Christ from the dead, and which raised the sinner from his death in sin, shall also raise up those who are Christ's to everlasting life.

As in the time of Zerubbabel the ruined temple was built, not by might, nor by power, but by the Spirit of God, much more now cannot the body of flesh become a temple of the Holy Ghost, and the spiritual temple of Christ on earth, His Church, go up, but by the Spirit of God. For its edification He gave apostles, teachers, helps, and divers gifts; and now Himself dwells in and works with it with divine power. Through His word and with His gifts and grace He is now making Christ's redemption effectual to the world. The Spirit and the Bride are now inviting all who will to come and take freely of the water of life.

From the words and works and lives of those who are filled with the Spirit, and upon whose ministry He is poured out with blessing, we may truly judge of the person and character and will and work of the Spirit Himself in His administration of the kingdom of Christ.

The Foreign Secretary of the American Board said, at one of its annual meetings, that he was accustomed to give to outgoing missionaries, as a complete manual of instructions, a copy of the Acts of the Apostles.

The Epistles are written to teach true doctrine and holy living, being about equally divided between both; requiring that the faith of Christ shall bring forth the fruits of the Spirit. The Christian should believe the words, live the life, and do the works of the Spirit.

And the messages of the Spirit to the seven churches of Asia are equally His messages to the churches to-day. He does not cease to keep before them the glory of the Son of God and to magnify Him in the midst of them. He knows their works and trials, and would give them the same counsels and admonitions, and the same encouragements and promises. The Church and the work of Christ are His care and delight, and Christians and their work are dearer to Him than all else of earth. He abides with them that they may continue faithful and fruitful.

If now it shall be asked, how we may know that any one is filled with the Spirit, and how any word or work is of the Spirit, the answer is at hand. He Himself bids us "try the spirits whether they be of God." And the first criterion is this, · Every spirit which confesseth that Jesus

Christ is come in the flesh is of God, and every spirit which confesseth not Jesus is not of God," is anti-Christ and anti-Holy Spirit. The whole work of the Spirit is in the name of Christ, and on no other ground than His atonement for sin does He have aught to do with or for sinners; and His administration is for the glory of Christ. He teaches the things of Christ; and "no man speaking by the Spirit of God calleth Jesus accursed, and no man can say that Jesus is the Lord but by the Holy Spirit. Whosoever believeth that Jesus is the Christ is born of God the Spirit. So also is he who loves the children of God, and he who keeps His commandments born of the Spirit."

The carnally-minded is at enmity with God, but he who minds the things of the Spirit has life and peace; and whosoever overcometh the world, gaining his victory through faith in Christ, is of the Spirit. The Spirit alone casts out devils, and in the name of Christ.

All the Christian graces are His fruits, and the evidences of His gracious work in the heart. He is the Spirit of truth, and Christ is *the* Truth. That which Christ is and manifested of God, what He said and promised, His Gospel, is emphatically and supremely the truth. And the interpretation of this truth of Christ must be according to the proportion or analogy of faith to be of the

Spirit. Faith in Jesus Christ is the one instrumental condition through which the Spirit communicates His efficacious grace.

We may try any spirit by his own words and works, by his spirit of love and obedience, and by his relation to Christ. This latter is the touchstone of all spiritual truth and life. All things are in the name of the Lord Jesus which are by the Spirit of God. To be filled with the Holy Spirit is to be filled with light and truth and love, with grace and strength and faith, with praise and joy and hope, with the indwelling and communion and blessing of the Spirit of Christ.

And this same mighty and blessed work of the Spirit of God has been manifest in every age of the Church; and to-day, more than ever before, the Gospel, preached by men filled with the Holy Spirit, is the power of God unto salvation.

Christianity is the one great, universal fact, and the ministration of the Spirit the one enlightening, moulding, and saving power of the world. A missionary goes forth, single-handed, and lays siege at the gate of a nation, and in the name of Christ sets up his banners, and conquers by the power of the Spirit; walls of ignorance and superstition and evil falling before the blast of his Gospel trumpet. And this work shall go on, more and more gloriously, until the Gospel shall be preached in all the world to every creature; until through the spread of the Church of Christ, filled with the Holy Spirit, the kingdoms of this earth shall become the kingdoms of our Lord and His Christ.

Christ's promise: "Lo, I am with you alway, even unto the end of the world," unto "the consummation of the ages," is fulfilled in the gift and presence and work of the Spirit.

CHAPTER V.

THE LOVE OF THE SPIRIT.

If one should be asked, "Do you love the Holy Spirit?" he would not have an answer ready as if the question were, "Do you love Jesus?" Or, if the question were, "Does the Holy Spirit love you?" would the answer be as certain as if it were, "Does God love you?"

Probably you have not got much beyond the Apostles' Creed, "I believe in the Holy Ghost"; or, if you have prayed for His presence as a Spirit of Power, you never have thought of Him as the Spirit of Love, who loves you personally with Divine love unspeakable.

You often have wished that you had lived when Christ was in the flesh. Could you see His face, and walk with Him in the way, and hear His words, and talk with Him, you would understand Him and believe Him and love Him, and would follow Him even unto death, forgetting how Peter and the other disciples forsook Him and fled. He said it was better for them, and for us, that He should go away, that the Comforter might

THE LOVE OF THE SPIRIT. 61

come, whom He would send to more than fill His place, and to be with us forever.

And His going by the way of the cross was the very condition of the Spirit's coming, the purchase of His blessing and ministry. Since then the Holy Spirit has dwelt personally with the Church, filling her that He might reveal and glorify Christ; and so He has been the efficient instrument in the upbuilding of the kingdom of Christ. Yet the Church has not given Him the welcome nor the honor that He merits, nor the equal place in her heart and her prayers that He deserves.

We pray for the Holy Spirit, we invoke His divine presence and almighty power, but seldom do we pray to Him personally and give Him thanks; much less do we express our love to Him, and ask Him to bestow His divine love upon us.

And in whatever way we have failed to exalt Him in our thoughts, or to love Him in our hearts, or to worship Him in our devotions, we have failed of receiving the fullness of His blessed fellowship.

The Church has yet very much to learn concerning the Holy Spirit; if, indeed, this is not the special department of divine knowledge and revelation which she needs just now to know experimentally, and in whose unveiling lies her still more glorious development.

While the Holy Spirit is divine power and wisdom and truth, He has equally all the divine attributes and perfections; but is, in a special manner in His relations to the Church, Divine Love; and until we know and worship Him as Divine Love we can hardly be said to know Him at all.

It is not only difficult, but in many respects it is impossible to distinguish the persons of the Godhead; and to take in this mystery of godliness is, of course, beyond the stretch of finite mind. It will ever be a growing mystery with increasing knowledge in the ages to come. Whenever we think of one, we cannot forget the other persons of the blessed Trinity; for in all divine revelations each strives to glorify the other, and each is equally interested in and glorified by the others' glory.

The Father, the Son, and the Holy Spirit promote, partake of, and enjoy one another's glory, and by their benevolence towards and complacency in one another exhibit the divine unity. In all their relations to us they manifest, not only their divine love for us, but also, and equally, their love for one another. And while it is not always easy to distinguish their personal love to us, so united are they in the work of our redemption, yet so marked is this as the characteristic of the Godhead, that we can only and fully express it by saying, God the Father is Divine Love, God the Son is Divine Love, and God the Spirit is Divine Love; and then gather all in one, and say, as does St. John, "God is love"; and he knows Him not in His fullness of divine love who loves not Father and Son and Holy Spirit.

There is, however, a clear distinction in their personal love to us, which is manifested in their offices and work, and which indicates their personal relations to us.

And while we have constantly dwelt on and rejoiced in the love of the Father and the love of the Son, have we thought sufficiently, if at all, of the love of the Spirit toward us?

Yet it is a blessed truth that the Spirit loves us equally with the Father and the Son, and is now doing a work of love for us as divine as theirs. It is, indeed, true that the love of the Father and the love of the Son are often mentioned in the Word of God, while the love of the Spirit, the Inspirer of the Scriptures, is mentioned directly but once; yet this agrees with what Christ taught concerning His work, "He shall not speak of Himself," "He shall glorify me." And in this He manifests a divine self-forgetfulness and benevolence, like that of Christ in the flesh, which subordinates His own glory to the glory of Christ.

In Romans xv. 30, where St. Paul mentions the love of the Spirit, he is speaking of "the fullness of the blessing of the Gospel of Christ"; and adds, "Now I beseech you, brethren, for our Lord Jesus Christ's sake and for the love of the Spirit, that ye strive together with me in your prayers to God for me," thus making the love of the Spirit and the glory of Christ equally strong inducements to faith and prayer.

The old adage, "Actions speak louder than words," applies to the Spirit's work of love above that of all others. Wherever the work of the Spirit is mentioned, and wherever it is seen, His love is implied or manifested. Love is everywhere its inspiration. The Acts of the Apostles, being those of men full of the Holy Spirit, show His love on every page of their record. And His administration of the Church in and since their day attests the same Divine Love.

No doctrine, therefore, can be more practical and profitable, for the Church to know by a living experience, than this of the Divine love of the Holy Spirit; and it should also be the joy of every Christian that his Teacher and Sanctifier and Comforter is Divine Love.

For the unfolding of this truth, the writer is greatly indebted to a work of an old English author, Rev. Robert Philip, entitled "The Love of the Spirit," which has been blessed not a little to his own Christian experience, and from which he will have occasion often to quote, since he cannot hope to improve upon the beauty and force of his words.

That the Love of the Spirit may be clearly seen in His work, it will be necessary to notice briefly the love of the Father and the love of the Son in the work of redemption. Man was fallen, ruined, and lost, without help or hope; justly condemned by the holy and righteous and good law of God; when the Divine love of the Father was so moved with compassion toward this apostate world that "He gave His only-begotten Son, that whosoever believeth on Him should not perish, but have everlasting life."

The Divine Son held the most intimate possible relation to the Father; and was the only-begotten, the only one He could give and not replace, and the only one who could pay the price of the world's redemption. Him the Father gave up to humiliation and death, laying the burden and penalty of the world's sin and guilt upon Him. "It pleased the Lord to bruise Him," so did He love us.

And when the Father asked for some one to become a substitute and sacrifice to bear the sins of the world and redeem it from its curse, the Divine Son also so loved us as to give Himself for us, saying, "Here am I; send me." He "came into the world to save sinners," and "while we were yet sinners Christ died for us."

He drank the bitter cup of our sins in sad Gethsemane, and poured out His soul unto death for us on Calvary; without which our salvation was impossible.

Thus He bought the privilege of proclaiming to the world, through the Spirit and the Church, salvation to the uttermost through Himself.

The love of Christ for us as that of the Father passeth knowledge—broad as the universe, long as eternity, deep as sin, and high as heaven.

But how did sinners treat His gift of saving grace, purchased at such a price? "Ye will not come unto me that ye might have life," Christ exclaims in an agony of disappointment. It was this rejection of His love that made him "a man of sorrows." His most pathetic wail over Jerusalem was only the prelude to His death of a broken heart on the cross, because man would not take His gift of love.

And no man of his own will ever has come to Christ for salvation; and except the Father draw Him by His Spirit none ever will be saved through Him. Did the Divine love end here all were lost, and the cross were vain to man. And nothing could show greater love before high heaven than to provide at such a sacrifice grace unto salvation for sinful man.

But the Divine love did not end here; the love of the Spirit is yet to be most gloriously revealed. The Father and the Son gave and sent Him to complete the work of redemption. There is now no more need of sacrifice and suffering; the price is paid, and redemption is free; but that the gift of Christ may become saving grace, it must become regenerating and sanctifying grace. The sinner must be convicted of his sin, and enabled to accept Christ as his Saviour; his heart must be renewed by the Holy Spirit; and then he must be sanctified until he shall be made meet for heaven. The Holy Spirit must give him entrance into the kingdom of heaven through Christ the way. Christ wrought salvation *for* the sinner; but the Spirit's work is further necessary to work salvation *in* the sinner—one is the complement of the other.

The love of the Spirit is just as necessary, in its place, to the salvation of a sinner as that of the Father and the Son; and it will detract nothing from their love to magnify the love of the Spirit, but will rather glorify it.

I cannot make this plainer than does Mr. Philip.* "The real question is now, What was wanted after Christ had finished His atoning work? There was His sacrifice, perfect, all-sufficient, and glorious! Nothing could be added to its merits, or its efficacy, or its acceptableness

---
* "Love of the Spirit," chap. i.

before God as a ransom for souls. But still around that sacrifice stood a world, yea, a Church, which knew neither its merits nor its meaning, and which never could have understood them had not the Spirit explained them, and never would have employed them had He not applied them. Thus, although the fountain for sin and uncleanness was opened by the death of Christ, there were none to wash their robes in the blood of the Lamb until the love of the Spirit enlightened and led them. But for His love, therefore, the love of Christ would have remained unappreciated and unknown both to the world and to the Church."

"But for what the Spirit did, all that Christ endured would have had no saving effect upon man. It is the very glory of the Saviour's love that it depended as much on the sanctifying love of the Spirit, as the paternal love did on the blood of the Lamb."

Dr. Wardlaw also well says: "The work of Christ and the work of the Spirit are mutually necessary to each other's efficacy; and are thus both alike indispensable to the salvation of a sinner. Without the work of Christ the Spirit would want the means, or the instrument of His operation; and without the work of the Spirit the means would remain inefficacious and fruitless."

The necessity of the work of the Spirit to the efficacy of the work of Christ could not be more strongly put than by St. Paul, when he says, "No man can say that Jesus is the Lord but by the Holy Spirit."

Concerning the motive of the Spirit's work, Dr. Owen says: "The principle or foundation of all the Spirit's actings for our consolation is His own infinite love and condescension. He willingly proceeded and came forth from the Father to be our Comforter. He knew what we were and what would be our dealings with Him. He knew we would grieve Him, provoke Him, quench His motion, defile His dwelling-place, and yet He would come to be our Comforter."

Thus the fullness of the Divine love appears only when we try to measure the love of the Father in planning, the love of the Son in procuring, and the love of the Spirit in applying redemption. The grace of God came from the Father, through the Son and by the Spirit, bringing salvation; originating in the love of the Father, made free by the love of the Son, and efficacious by the love of the Spirit. The Father shows His love by what He gave; the Son His love in what He suffered, and the Spirit His love in what He does; and this is intensified beyond measure by the fact, that it is Divine love for the ungodly, for sinners, for the enemies of God.

The love of the Father and the Son also sent the Spirit into the world, that He should, with His own Divine love and power and grace, be our personal Comforter, to dwell and work in and with us forever.

The Father's love was infinite benevolence, divinest compassion toward a perishing world; deserving to perish as sinners against His holy law. For the same sinners, and while they were yet sinners, Christ died, the just for the unjust, love passing knowledge. To the same sinners the Holy Spirit came and gave Himself to abide with them.

The incarnation of the Son of God, with His humiliation and suffering in the flesh, is the great mystery of godliness. For three-and-thirty years He lived on this earth, buffeted of Satan and disowned and despised and rejected of men; when He rose from the dead: ascended into heaven, and is now at the right hand of the Majesty on high, our ever-living Intercessor.

Is it not also a like humiliation for the Holy Spirit to come from Heaven to earth to live with and dwell in sinful flesh to the end of the world? The association with and contradiction of sinners which Christ endured so meekly a few years, the Spirit endures continually in His love for Christ and for us. This appears still more vividly when we consider that the Spirit is the Holy

Spirit; holy in His nature and character, and will and work; infinitely delighting in holiness and utterly abhorring sin; the giver and executor of the holy law; the very conscience of the Godhead itself; who could not look upon sin, or do aught but take holy vengeance upon it, except through the blood of Christ; who also approved of Christ as a sin-offering before ever He would undertake to atone for man's guilt or bear its penalty. Conceive of what it would be for the saintliest man of earth to go into a saloon and stay there in association with the intemperate; amidst the smoke of tobacco and the fumes of liquor; obliged to listen to the coarse blasphemy and the disgusting vileness of its inmates, and we get a faint idea of what it means for the Holy Spirit to come to strive with sinful man even to save him.

For Him to have anything to do with sin, to be where it is, to dwell in the midst of it, to show it any favor, would be infinite condescension and boundless love.

He who finally destroys forever from the presence of the Lord and the glory of His power sinners out of Christ; preserving and maintaining eternally the purity of holy heaven; yet comes to this sinful and accursed earth to abide; the very last place, in the universe of God, where we would expect to find the Holy Spirit, except it were in hell itself; and sinful earth must be as a hell to Him.

The sacrifice of Christ was the only condition on which He could or would sanction the offer of pardon and grace to sinners; and only in Christ's name does He come to a sinner to offer or bestow grace. And what makes the love of the Holy Spirit more remarkable, is the fact, that He knew into just what kind of a world He was coming. He knew the nature of the carnal heart; its disobedience to the holy law; its deceitfulness and desperate wickedness; its enmity against God and all good. He knew how Christ was despised and rejected of men; and put to death by those He came to save, and that He Himself would receive exactly the same treatment. As it is not possible to conceive of admitting sin into holy heaven and its remaining holy and God's throne and dwelling-place, no more can we conceive how the Holy Spirit can endure to dwell in this sinful world, and not destroy its sin with immediate destruction. Nor can sinful man himself conceive of the exceeding sinfulness of his sin. Only the Holy Spirit can reveal its evil and desert; and His measure of it is only partly conveyed to us by the everlasting penalty of the law, and the infinite sacrifice of Christ. The very holiness of the Spirit conceals His love while it reveals it; as the light blinds our eyes with its

THE LOVE OF THE SPIRIT. 73

very purity so that we forget that it also gives light and warmth.

It is a wonder of wonders that the Holy Spirit ever comes to a sinner and has any dealings with him except to execute judgment.

It is a still greater wonder that He stays so long and waits so patiently; and it is a miracle of love, Divine love and grace, that He makes a sinful heart a fit temple for His indwelling here, and meet for the fellowship of heaven hereafter.

And He comes, not only to the worthiest and best, but even to the chief of sinners, and undertakes to save the worst and the vilest. And this He does without being under any personal obligation or necessity; and when it seems almost to be unholy; the moving of it being altogether apart from man; and from His own divine benevolence; made possible by the love and righteousness of Christ.

In all this work, He is a free Spirit, and His work is one of personal, Divine love.

And He is not grieved away, nor quenched; but stays and works, for weeks and months and years, until love has conquered sin, and the sinner has become a saint, and the saint is glorified in Christ.

The long-suffering patience of the Holy Spirit with the sinner is infinite forbearance and kindness, and His patience with the saints is also the patience of Divine love unwearied.

Owen, in his work on "Spiritual-Mindedness," says that "the thoughts of spiritual things are with many as guests that come into an inn, and not like children that dwell in the house." His guests come and go and are entertained for a time and forgotten; and the innkeeper knows little of them, having no personal interest in them, and entertains all alike courteously. If a great or a royal one comes, unannounced, he is treated like others, and at times angels are entertained unawares. The Holy Spirit comes into the heart unrecognized; or instead of being given a place to dwell, or welcomed even as a guest, is turned away, not as a stranger, but as an enemy; or, if He must be admitted for a time, is given a place with one's worldly thoughts instead of a sanctuary. The Lord is in the heart and is unknown. A more than angelic messenger and minister, who comes with glad tidings and would stay and bless with all Divine blessings, is turned away, neglected, grieved, and provoked, it may be so as never to return again. Engrossed with the trifles and vanities of earth, God is forgotten and heaven is lost.

"What but love," exclaims Mr. Philip,[*] "could

---

[*] "Love of the Spirit," chap. i.

THE LOVE OF THE SPIRIT. 75

have induced the Holy Spirit to strive with us at all? and He might justly have passed us by when we first resisted Him. Did He not love equally with the Father and the Son, He never would have tried to make a holy temple of your heart and mine."

Open wide your hearts, beloved, to the love of the Spirit; watch eagerly for His coming, and give Him a joyful welcome; listen eagerly to His sweet pleadings, and make Him a sanctuary. Dwell in His blessed fellowship, and grieve Him not for your life; and, when He convicts of sin, depart from it at any cost; when He takes of the things of Christ, and shows them unto you, accept them with all your hearts, that He may apply them to your salvation and sanctification.

What better thing can one ask for you than that the love of the Holy Spirit may be with you.

CHAPTER VI.

THE LOVE OF THE SPIRIT IN CONVICTING OF SIN.

HAVING considered the love of God, that the Father is Divine Love, and the Son is Divine Love, and the Spirit is Divine Love, and how each of the Blessed Three personally manifests the Divine Love to us—the Father in what He gave, the Son in what He suffered, and the Spirit in what He does—we shall be ready to give to the Holy Spirit His equal place, and to notice in particular the works which manifest His personal love to us in His present and personal administration of the kingdom of heaven.

Our Lord promised to send the Spirit to be our present and personal divine Comforter, and told us how He should perform this gracious office. "And when He is come He will reprove," or convict, "the world of sin and of righteousness and of judgment."

A strange way this, it would seem at first thought, to help and comfort, and not so much to manifest love as severity.

The word "convict," which is the rendering of

the revised version, gives us the true idea of His work. He does more than to reprove the world; He convicts it.

This shows no approbation of or sympathy with sin, but condemnation of it; and is generally a most thankless office.

Few have the moral courage, not to speak of the love, to tell even their dearest friends their faults, and point out to them faithfully but kindly their sins; and fewer still will receive such reproof in a spirit of meekness.

Not many can say with the Psalmist: "Let the righteous smite me, and it shall be a kindness. Let him reprove me, and it shall be an excellent oil which shall not break my head." To give or to receive such a reproof in the right spirit is a distinguishing grace. But simply to reprove the world of sin is not worthy of the Comforter, and does not take the place of Christ's personal presence.

Archdeacon Hare, in his " Mission of the Comforter," says : * " We did not need that the Spirit of God should come down from heaven to reprove the world of sin—the words of men would have been sufficient for this."

The Holy Spirit knew sin in its Satanic nature, in its vileness and deadly wickedness, and

---

* p. 36.

sought nothing less than its utter destruction. He would exterminate it root and branch.

He knew that the heart of man was carnal, and would mind the things of the flesh; was enmity against God, and would not be subject to His law. He saw the choice, the will, the affections, the conscience, the very nature of man depraved, needing not only light, but life. Christ had come, and had been despised and rejected and put to death by those He came to save.

Vain would have been His coming and His love had not the Spirit been sent for a greater work than reproof or warning or invitation. The love of Christ had already done all this. The Spirit came to *convict* the world of sin, and this conviction was not merely to make the world know its sin—this it already knew—but to convict with reference to an end worthy of His coming; to convict unto repentance and salvation; to convict of sin *because they believed not on Christ*, and that they should believe on Him.

His work of conviction was a means, not an end. It looked Christward and was for His glory. Christ was "the way and the truth and the life," and the Spirit would lead the sinner in the way, through the truth, to the life in Christ. In the hands even of the Spirit the Law is a law of sin and death, and He has no law of life except in Christ Jesus.

Mr. Philip says :* "There is no conversion from sin until there be conviction of sin ; and there is no conviction of sin which tends to Christ or to holiness, but that which the Holy Spirit plants in the soul."

Christ's death was the divinest expression of the sinfulness and ruin of sin and of man's perishing need of mercy. This was the precious price of redemption. Man was condemned already, and neither Christ nor the Spirit came to show this, but that he might be saved. And now that Christ has died, the sinner's condemnation is because he will not believe on Him. The Spirit came for, and is intent on, producing conviction of this one sin of unbelief and rejection of Christ. Even His divine love would not have brought Him to the world for any other purpose. He could not convict with any promise of peace or help or hope except through Christ. Like Him He came into the world to save sinners.

See now the love of the Spirit as He condescends to us sinners, searching the heart, piercing it with truth, troubling conscience, reproving, threatening, condemning, showing delusions, stripping off self-righteousness ; while we are provoked at Him and hate Him for it, and quench Him and grieve Him more and more ; His pure eyes beholding the vileness of our sin, the stench of it

---

* "Love of the Spirit," chap. ii.

coming up into His nostrils, its profanity and blasphemy filling His ears; yet with divine long-suffering and infinite compassion He tells us faithfully the truth and leaves us not, but comes again and again, for months and years, even down to old age, that He may lead us to repentance and reception of Christ.

In all this He is a faithful friend, a true comforter, never deceiving with false hopes, never speaking peace to the wicked, pointing always and only to Christ. But for Christ's redemption He could not do this; but for His own great love He would not, and for our sakes He does it that we may live and not die.

The sin of unbelief is that for which finally the impenitent perish. All other sins culminate in this which rejects Christ. For other sins there is hope until this last hope is cut off. Unbelief in Christ is also and equally rejection of the love of the Father and of the Holy Spirit.

The law punishes sin against its commandments with severity. "Of how much sorer punishment," says the Epistle to the Hebrews, "shall he be thought worthy who hath trodden under-foot the Son of God, and hath counted the blood of the covenant wherewith he was sanctified an unholy thing and hath done despite to the Spirit of grace?" He shall fall into the hands of the living God, who taketh vengeance.

Having convinced us of sin, until we see and feel its guilt and danger, and are ready humbly to confess it and to turn from it with hatred of it, until perhaps we so feel our helpless and lost condition that we know not how such a sinner can be saved, the Spirit takes of the things of Christ and shows them unto us, making Him all-glorious as a Saviour.

This is the second step in His work of conviction, to testify of the righteousness of Christ, who is gone to the Father, having finished the work given Him to do, and is become our Mediator.

As the sinner has no true sense of his sin until the Spirit convinces him of it, so he cannot know the purity of righteousness and the beauty of holiness, or appreciate the righteousness of Christ, and will not care for a part in His imputed righteousness who bore the penalty of his sin until taught of the Spirit. He does not see that his own righteousnesses are as "filthy rags," and that his self-righteousness only plunges him deeper and deeper into the mire, until the Spirit, in His faithful love, makes him to see his uncleanness.

Not until then can the Spirit present the righteousness of Christ with any success. And He is not such a Comforter that He will be content with any half-way work, with simply producing "the sorrow of the world," which acts from fear of consequences, and not from conviction of the sinfulness of sin and the need of Christ's righteousness; but will work that repentance which is Godly sorrow, which turns from sin and seeks the mercy of God.

Nothing shows more clearly the long-suffering, the patient, the inexhaustible love of the Spirit in convicting of the sin of unbelief and of the need of Christ's righteousness, than to consider the classes of sinners to which He comes and the changes He works in them, as given by St. Paul: " Know you not that the unrighteous shall not inherit the kingdom of God? Be not deceived, neither fornicators, nor idolaters, nor adulterers, nor effeminate, nor abusers of themselves with mankind, nor thieves, nor covetous, nor drunkards, nor revilers, nor extortioners shall inherit the kingdom of God. And *such were some of you*, but ye are washed, but ye are sanctified, but ye are justified in the name of the Lord Jesus and by the Spirit of our God."

The Spirit goes to the lowest and vilest and worst, and brings them into the kingdom of God.

Again, while "the flesh lusteth against the Spirit," and " the works of the flesh are adultery, fornication, uncleanness, lasciviousness, idolatry, sorcery, enmities, strife, jealousies, wrath, factions, divisions, heresies, envyings, drunkenness, revellings, and such like," He comes to the flesh and works conviction and repentance until it is changed

HIS LOVE IN CONVICTING OF SIN.

to bring forth the fruits of "love, joy, peace, long-suffering, gentleness, goodness, faithfulness, meekness, and temperance," the works of righteousness.

Even to the apostle who wrote these things, and when he was breathing out threatenings and slaughter against the disciples of the Lord and persecuting Him, the Spirit came; not in vengeance, but in convicting love, removing the scales from Saul's blind eyes, until it was said of Him, "behold, he prayeth"; and afterwards Paul presents himself to the world as an example of the divine long-suffering and mercy.

The Spirit comes by the still small voice; and if the sinner will not listen to that, He comes with a startling providence, or severe affliction; and at times when the sinner is most desperate in sin and in places where we would least expect the Holy Spirit to go, He goes a faithful Comforter seeking to save.

No mother was ever so patient with a disobedient child, no father ever so grieved over a prodigal son, no wife ever so bore with a drunken husband as the Spirit of God bears with rebellious and hardened and lost sinners.

To know and receive Him when He comes in conviction is the very first step in the way of salvation. By this means He is seeking to stop sinners in the road to destruction; and to arrest their thoughts and turn them to Christ.

Let one receive Him in conviction and the Spirit will soon lead him to Christ, working repentance of sin, and faith in Christ's blood and righteousness.

Now, if one goes to Christ as the Spirit leads and seeks mercy in His name, the Spirit not only has authority and power to grant it, but takes greatest delight in answering his prayer. He can and will do all things for any sinner who asks in Jesus' name.

By His own almighty power and in His own mysterious way, the Spirit creates in him a clean heart and renews a right spirit within him.

The sinner experiences " the washing of regeneration and the renewing of the Holy Ghost," and becomes "a new creature in Christ Jesus."

Being now washed from sin the Spirit can take complacent delight in him; and being also united to Christ, having become a partaker of His grace, the Spirit loves him even as he loves Christ, whose he now is. And here His love seems to change entirely, and besides being long-suffering and compassionate and convicting, is also joyful and personal, and approving and complacent. He sheds abroad in the sinner's heart the love of God and bears witness to his pardon. The change is in the sinner and not in the Holy Spirit.

Now, the Spirit manifests the same love in his justification, not only by showing the things of

Christ unto him, but by applying them to his pardon and acceptance as righteous. The Spirit's love glows and beams as with a flame as He witnesses to the sinner that his sins are forgiven and he is reconciled to God.

He speaks peace to his conscience and gives him joy in the hope of the glory of God, while He admits him to all the rights and privileges of the sons of God.

And when the Spirit sheds abroad the love of God in his heart, the believer experiences a new-born love which realizes for the first time that God is love and sees Christ as " the chiefest among ten thousand," and " altogether lovely."

All his spiritual powers are quickened and ruled by the love of God; humility and penitence and faith are mingled with peace and joy and hope, while sin is crucified and righteousness is chosen and loved. The Holy Spirit is a welcome guest where once the door was shut to Him. His presence gives unspeakable joy and comfort and His fellowship is esteemed the choicest friendship.

Thus it is evident that it is as the Spirit of Truth that the Holy Spirit is our real Comforter.

Christ, as God manifest in the flesh, is the Truth, who purchases and proclaims redemption in comparison with which nothing else is truth to man.

To know God, and Jesus Christ whom He hath sent, is prime truth and all knowledge, even eternal life. Christ is all and in all.

And the Spirit is also the Truth in revealing Christ to us, in convincing us of the sin of unbelief as our great sin, and of the righteousness of Christ as the only ground and hope of our salvation.

When, therefore, you ask of the Spirit of God, "What is truth?" His answer is, "Christ is the Truth." He is, as He said, "the way, the truth, and the life." No man cometh to the Father but by Him. The washing of regeneration and renewing of the Holy Ghost is poured on us richly through Jesus Christ our Saviour.

And the Church in her ministry of reconciliation has borne her witness that, "God was in Christ reconciling the world unto Himself, not imputing their trespasses unto them," and "hath made Him to be sin for us who knew no sin, that we might be made the righteousness of God in Him."

And in further convincing the world " of judgment, because the prince of this world hath been judged," the Spirit shows the benefit of the righteousness of Christ and its acceptance with the Father and Himself as a ground of justification for those who trust in it; and also how Christ is the righteous judge who shall crown with righteousness them that believe on Him; and reward the saints with eternal life; and so shall His kingdom be established forever.

In his masterpiece of strategy, in the temptation in the wilderness, Satan was repulsed by Christ through His faith in God and obedience to His will. So again in his master-stroke of malignity, whereby he thought to destroy His kingdom and prevent the salvation of the world, by accomplishing Christ's death, Satan only established the righteousness of Christ forever, and gave Him an inviolable title to His kingdom; and secured the purchase of redemption for all who shall believe in Him.

They who are in Christ need have no fear of Satan's utmost attacks on them, when Christ in whom they trust has been the death of death; slaying their last enemy and giving victory forever to the saints.

In His judgment every knee shall bow, and every tongue confess that Jesus is the Christ to the glory of God the Father.

Of this also the Spirit convinces them who trust in the righteousness of Christ, when He speaks peace to them and assures them of the hope of the glory of God, enabling them to say "Abba, Father." Whom He justifies, them He will also glorify. Nothing shall separate them from the love of God which is in Christ Jesus our Lord

But for the love of God the Father, in sending Christ, the world had perished without help or hope.

But for the love of Christ in giving up His life to provide a righteousness for us, we had remained under condemnation and "dead in trespasses and sins."

And but for the same infinite love of the Spirit we would inevitably have perished in our sin and hardness and unbelief, and have been lost in the very sight of the cross. The way to heaven would have been made with none to walk in it, and the gate of heaven open with none to enter in.

Thus the great love of the Spirit in conviction is manifest in the end He seeks by it, the salvation of the sinner and the glory of Christ. Nor does His love end when He has brought the sinner to Christ, penitent and justified, but has only just begun. He has only introduced him to Christ, the way; and will, with the same patient, faithful Divine love, be his Comforter until the end is consummated in glory. And although His love seems to be different after He begins to bestow the grace of Christ upon the sinner, it is the same.

He did not convict the sinner to taunt him with his sins and condemnation, and to make him wretched, but to bring him to Christ; and now He abides with him in whom He has begun a good work, to sanctify him and make him complete in Christ. The Christian has only just begun to drink of the fountain of His divine love.

When the man of God goes into a saloon, or a gambling-hell, or brothel, we know that nothing but love for their wretched inmates takes him there, and his object is their salvation; while his very presence there produces conviction of sin and shame, and is as light in darkness; and we call his spirit one of Christian compassion and heaven-born charity. It is angelic, yea! Christ-like work.

So, for the Holy Spirit to come to this lost world to convict it of sin, to abide and suffer long and wait to save, is even better for us than to have Christ with us in the body.

Blot out from the earth all the sweet ministries of love, born of the Spirit in Christian charity, and this world were a wilderness and a desert of sin and death. Had not the Holy Spirit come to earth with His convicting, comforting, saving love and grace, blackness of darkness had settled down upon it in an everlasting night of death and despair.

Surely the Spirit of God is the Comforter divinely sent, and is Himself Divine love, and as an ever-present Christ.

CHAPTER VII.

THE LOVE OF THE SPIRIT IN SANCTIFICATION.

GREAT as is the love of the Spirit in convicting us of sin, His love does not end with this; indeed, He has only just begun to manifest it and we to experience it. The Holy Spirit will not leave us until He has made us holy like Himself.

Paul writes to the Corinthians as "unto them that are sanctified in Christ Jesus, called to be saints"; and to the Thessalonians, "The very God of peace sanctify you wholly." Peter writes to Christians as "elect through sanctification of the Spirit."

This shows the further work which remains to be done by the Spirit until we shall become saints indeed, fitted for glory. Christ, who has been made unto us wisdom and righteousness, is yet to be made unto sanctification and redemption before our salvation shall be completed. We were washed and justified, now we are to be sanctified, in the name of the Lord Jesus and by the Spirit of our God.

As Christ was our justification and the Spirit

our Justifier, so also is Christ our sanctification and the Spirit our Sanctifier.

We who were born of the Spirit are spirit; who were carnally-minded are spiritually-minded. We walk not after the flesh, but after the Spirit; are not under the law of sin and death, but under the law of the Spirit of life in Christ Jesus. We are new creatures in Christ, yet as new-born babes in Him, crying for light, needing the sincere milk of the Word; learning to walk, we are to grow up to youth and manhood and a ripe spiritual age, as from the blade to the ear and to the full corn in the ear. Having been made partakers of the imputed and justifying righteousness of Christ, we are to become really and personally and practically righteous.

As babes and children need constantly a mother's care, so we need the instruction and guidance and strengthening and comfort of the loving Spirit.

While our conviction of sin and of righteousness may have been a long and gradual process, our regeneration and justification were immediate; our sanctification being, as the word implies, also a process of the Spirit, a making holy, to continue while we are in the flesh.

Yet it will not be improper, and will simplify our idea of it, to regard the whole work of the Spirit, from conviction of sin to glorification, as the one work of sanctification; the regeneration being the crisis of the work; that without which nothing more could be done.

In regeneration, when the choice is made of holiness, one becomes spiritual, and whether the change seems gradual or sudden, the whole work must be attributed to the power and love of the Spirit.

It was not in the nature or desire or will of the carnal heart to change; so that where we find any hatred of sin and desire for holiness, any love for Christ or other fruits of the Spirit, we need not hesitate to ascribe them to the Spirit, or to say of one who bears them that he is born of the Spirit.*

But we would not expect a child to be as a man, so we should not look for perfection in the regenerate. He is a new creature and complete in Christ, yet very imperfect in himself. While a Christian is renewed in heart and purpose and affection, and has begun a spiritual life, he has the same body with its appetites and passions, and the same mind with its desires, that he had before conversion. And the mind and will and affections are not easily turned from the old ways of thinking and feeling and action, and the habits of years are not quickly changed. And no old facul-

---

* "Summer at Peace Cottage," chap. xxii.

ties are removed, nor are any new powers added by regeneration.

The old servants of sin must be taught and trained in the way of righteousness, and this will not be an easy or rapid process, but comes of long discipline and much experience. The flesh lusteth against the Spirit, sin dwelleth in him, evil is present when he would do good, the old man of sin dies hard, and there goes on an internal warfare in which one is often brought into captivity to the flesh. The natural disposition will be the same, but will be turned into holy channels, and easily-besetting sins will be the enemies to be watched and fought against. But there will be this marked difference, that now one does not allow, nor love, nor glory in sin, but grieves over it and strives to overcome it.

On the other hand, that which was good will become better, the gentleman will be more gentle, the sympathetic more tender, the benevolent more charitable, and the moral more upright. Each in his place and work will be better for having become a Christian.

Mr. Goulbourn speaks thus encouragingly of this beginning: "The more earnest desire for a holier life, which is often found in the soul, is something, nay, it is much, it is the fruit of grace; earnest desire of holiness is holiness in the germ thereof. Soon shalt thou know if thou *follow* on to know the Lord. But take one short and plain caution before we start. Sanctification is not the work of a day, but of a life. Growth in grace is subject to the same law of gradual and imperceptible advance as growth in nature." *

Let no one think that this process will be an easy one, or that sin can be overcome in any other way than by the constant help of the Holy Spirit. And this shows the great love of the Spirit, that in addition to all He has done for us in bringing us to Christ, He has undertaken our sanctification. And as this is like in character to His previous work, so it is to be accomplished by the same means. As we were justified through faith in Christ, and in His name, so we are to continue in union with Him by a life of faith for sanctification. And in all this work the Spirit is our most faithful and loving friend and comforter. There is, however, this difference, that, whereas formerly the heart was carnal, and He found nothing to please and could only convict of sin; now it is spiritual, and He comes into it with approving and complacent love; to convict still of sin, if sin remains, and to grieve over its backsliding and unbelief if it departs from Christ. He knows how weak we are, how prone to sin; but, instead of casting us off, would be our Paraclete or Standby and Helper.

---

* "Thoughts on Personal Religion," p. 13.

As He shed abroad the love of Christ in our hearts at conversion, so that we were ravished with His love, so He would more and more reveal Christ's love in its breadth and depth and length and height that we may know and partake of its fullness. His convicting faithfulness and regenerating power and grace and witness of justification are but foretastes of what He will do for us—the first-fruits and earnest of the Spirit, the pledge of our sanctification.

The first office-work of the Spirit after uniting us to Christ is that of Adoption. "To them that receive Christ He gives the power or right to become the sons of God, even to them that believe on His name. Led by the Spirit of God, they are the sons of God; minding the things of the Spirit, they show the work of the Spirit in their hearts. Now they receive the Spirit of adoption whereby they cry, Abba, Father." "The Spirit Himself beareth witness with our spirit that we are children of God; and if children, then heirs, heirs of God and joint heirs with Christ, if so be that we suffer with Him that we may also be glorified together."

An incident is at hand which shows what the Spirit undertakes in our adoption.*

Jim, a street-arab, a little bootblack of five

---

* *Illustrated Christian Weekly*, "Adopted Jim."

years, had attracted the attention of a benevolent woman, who finally said to him: "I want you to go home with me and be my boy. You shall have my name, and I will adopt you. Will you go?" He knew where she lived, and had often wished to have such a home; but now it was not easy to leave his old companions and give up his old life; yet with a strong resolution he said he would go. He was told that he was to put off his old ways and adopt her ways, and take her for his mother. But his old companions did not let him go to and fro without jeers and insults, until one day his temper gave way entirely, and he fought with them and became again as torn and dirty as when a bootblack. Then he said: "It's of no use. I'll not go home again. I'm only Jim, after all." Not so the mother, who went after him, and said in reply to his refusal to go back: "James, I adopted you. I have taken you into the family; I have given you my name. You are my heir. I love you." She took him home again, and he said: "I'm not Jim, after all, and will try harder to please."

So the Spirit, not once or twice, but as often as needs be, witnesses to our adoption.

When one is adopted as a son of God, his citizenship is in heaven. He is to live as a son, to be subject to the laws and grow into the ways of the Spirit, and to that end receive the discipline of a son.

He cannot any longer live after the flesh, but must mortify the deeds of the body and live after the Spirit. There cannot be life and peace, harmony within oneself and with his divine relations, unless there be spiritual-mindedness. In order to sanctification one must mind and love the things of the Spirit. And the Spirit dwells in the spiritual; but if carnality be there, He will change it to spirituality, or else move out of its presence.

It is to be particularly noticed that the Spirit which dwells in us is the Spirit of Christ, and that it is through our union with Christ that we are to grow in Christ-likeness.

As the branch abides in the vine, so we abide in Christ; and this is expressed by our faith, but the vital power by which we bear fruit is of the Spirit. Growth is the evidence of spiritual life, and faith in Christ is the condition and means of growth. Paul lived by the faith of the Son of God. We shall not therefore grow by our own struggles, but through faith. The life of the branch comes from the vine; and severed from it, the branch dies. A stone cannot of itself enter into the life of a plant, or a plant into that of an animal or of a man, except the higher life reaches down and appropriates and lifts up and assimilates the lower, and that by its own vital power; so the carnal does not become spiritual except as the Spirit converts it into His mind and service.

The law of life is the Spirit's law of sanctification or spiritual growth. All growth of the higher life is through the death of the life below it, by which it is nourished.

Mr. Drummond makes clear this process, where he says:* "The methods by which the spiritual man is to withdraw himself from the old environment, or from that part of it which will directly hinder the spiritual life, are three in number. First, suicide; second, mortification; third, limitation. These meet the different kinds of temptation. . . . . In suicide he must 'die unto sin,' and if he does not kill sin, sin will inevitably kill him. There are many sins which must be dealt with suddenly, or not at all. These are generally of the appetites and passions. . . . . If thine appetite offend thee, cut it off. Fatal desire in one organ will pay the penalty of life." Here there needs to be for safety total abstinence.

As to mortification, St. Paul says: "If ye through the Spirit do mortify the deeds of the body, ye shall live"; and beseeches, "Present your bodies a living sacrifice, holy, acceptable unto God." It requires watchfulness and long discipline to bring the body under. With refer-

---

* "Natural Law in the Spiritual World," p. 182.

ence to the desires of the mind, such as for wealth and learning and honor and power, there must be limitation at the point where they cease to serve the higher life. Beyond this they do injury and become sinful.

And with reference to the world, the same apostle also beseeches, " Be not conformed to this world, but be ye transformed by the renewing of your mind, that ye may prove what is that good and acceptable and perfect will of God." This metamorphosis from the worldly to the spiritual is of the Spirit. While the branch is joined to the vine for its life, it has also to do with the wind and rain and sun in its life and growth. One must fight the good fight of faith and lay hold on eternal life. And while without Christ and the Spirit he can do nothing, he can do all things through their help!

Our Saviour made the condition of discipleship that one should deny himself and take up his cross; which gives the method of sanctification; self-denial of whatever hinders spirituality, cross-bearing of whatever promotes it; obedience to the law becoming easier as one progresses in sanctification until it becomes a delight.

The precious eighth chapter of Romans meets the Christian at the point where he needs encouragement and help in fighting the old man of sin, and gives assurance of hope and of perseverance unto victory. Being freed from condemnation and under the law of the Spirit, of life in Christ Jesus; and having become spiritually-minded, he receives the adoption of a son and is an heir of God. Yet he suffers with Christ, but these sufferings are for a purpose, even his sanctification; that he may be fitted for glory with Christ. He shall be delivered from the bondage of corruption into the glorious liberty of the children of God. All the time he has the help and comfort of the Spirit, who will make all things work together for his good; and having predestinated and called and justified him, will also glorify him. God who spared not His own Son will with Him also, through the Spirit, freely give His saint all things, and nothing shall be able to separate him from the love of God. Who but the Spirit could defend him from all his enemies, and keep him united to Christ until his sanctification is completed?

It may seem strange that sufferings should be mentioned immediately after the witness of the Spirit to sonship. These sufferings are of the creature and are necessary for its deliverance from the bondage of corruption; and are like the trials and afflictions which beset the children of Israel in the wilderness, when the Lord delivered them from the bondage of Egypt and led them to Canaan.

They came not from the Lord nor from the way, but from their own unbelief and hardness of heart. The Lord would have given them immediate entrance into the land of promise had they been ready for it or willing to enter it; but the long wilderness wandering was a necessary discipline to wean them from idolatry and to fit them to occupy the land for Him.

The Spirit would spare us from trial and would give us blessings as fast as we are ready to receive them and as many as we are fitted to enjoy. All the good in Christ comes through our growth in grace; and our holiness is the measure of our receptivity; so that the Spirit is only good in using whatever means are necessary for our sanctification. He loves us in discipline even more than in blessing, and loves us too well to allow us to be led astray from Christ by the world or the flesh or the evil one; His love is manifest in taking away as well as in giving.

Mr. Philip says : * " His work is in tender love when we suspect Him of desertion and denial. .... Some think nothing love but comfort, nothing sympathy but consolation, and as these seem incompatible, they are ready to conclude that they are unconverted and thus not loved by the Spirit at all. They are wrong, sadly wrong, in thus suspecting the heart or the hand of the all-gracious Spirit; but as the Spirit of life in

---

* "Love of the Spirit," chap. v.

Christ Jesus He must give death-wounds to the love of sin and to the pride of the heart and to the power of self-righteousness. It is not the *begun* work of the Holy Spirit on the heart; but the finished work of Christ on the cross that gives real comfort." Again he says:* "The Holy Spirit will not wink at sin, nor connive at sloth, nor overlook worldly-mindedness. It is His great object to cure these faults and therefore He must convict us for them instead of consoling us under them. And this is true kindness as well as real prudence."

A faith in Jesus Christ for salvation will stand any test which can be brought upon it through the world or the flesh; and the Spirit would not have us deceived, nor will He allow us to be tried beyond our ability. St. Paul writes: "We glory in tribulation, knowing that tribulation worketh patience; and patience, proof or a test; and proof, hope; and hope maketh not ashamed, because the love of God hath been shed abroad in our hearts by the Holy Spirit which hath been given to us." The object of this tribulation is our sanctification, and is wisely as well as lovingly permitted.

And Peter writes of "the elect through sanctification of the Spirit," that they are "kept through the power of God," and if in "heaviness through

---

* Chap. xiii.

manifold temptations"; yet it is that the "test of their faith, more precious than gold, may be found unto praise and honor and glory at the appearing of Christ Jesus." The help as the joy of those in heaviness is in the Holy Spirit. He searches our hearts and reveals the hidden evil, not that He may discourage us, but that He may lead us to forsake the sin and look away to Christ for forgiveness and peace. Our doubts and fears arise from ourselves, and not from looking up to Christ.

Cheer up, then, ye fainting and fearful ones. Your very faintness and fears are evidences of the Spirit's loving patience, and show that He stands ready to help; and you may rest in the assurance that He who has begun a good work in you will continue it until the day of Jesus Christ.

"The natural man receiveth not the things of the Spirit of God; neither can he know them, because they are spiritually discerned." "Eye hath not seen, nor ear heard, neither have entered into the heart of man"—the natural man—"the things which God hath prepared for them that love Him. But God hath revealed them to us by His Spirit."

By such spiritual illumination and revelation of the things of God, blessed and glorious, the Spirit would also lead us from the world and sin to Christ and to the glory of the saints.

CHAPTER VIII.

THE SPIRIT A COMFORTER.

On His way to Gethsemane and Calvary our Lord forgot Himself in seeking to comfort His disciples; and even in the garden, while Himself drinking the bitter cup, He excused the weakness of their flesh.

Their hearts were sore troubled because He was going away, and He assures them with the promise: "I will not leave you comfortless. I will come unto you"; and "I will pray the Father, and He shall give you another Comforter that He may abide with you forever." The word "Comforter" is marginally rendered Helper or Standby, indicating present help and strength and comfort.

"It is expedient for you," says Christ, "that I should go away, for if I go not away the Comforter will not come unto you; but if I go I will send Him unto you."

By the Spirit He comes and abides with us. And for the glory of Christ and for the great love He Himself has for us, the Spirit comes to be our Comforter. There was none other, in heaven or in earth, who could take the place of Jesus.

He alone had the knowledge and strength and love and patience necessary for our weakness and waywardness and need. He knew our hearts and what we lacked and needed as well as Jesus did. Jesus kept His disciples in the Father's name; now we are to be "kept for Jesus Christ" by the Spirit. And we may be persuaded that He is able to keep that which we have committed to Him, when our Saviour has also and first committed our keeping to Him. A keep is a stronghold, high and secure, and the Spirit is now our refuge and strength, a very present help in trouble.

The last prayer of our Lord for His disciples would ask for them what was important for their good, and this was: "I pray not that Thou shouldest take them out of the world, but that Thou shouldest keep them from the evil one." In the simple prayer, which He taught them for daily use, they are to pray: "Lead us not into temptation, but deliver us from the evil one."

"Spare us from unnecessary trial, and guard from the power of Satan." What we call mysterious providences might be very plain if we knew the deceitfulness of sin or saw through the wiles of the devil. He who tried to seduce Christ

Himself when He was an hungered in the wilderness, will also take us at every disadvantage and attack us in our weakest spot; will tempt our appetite, flatter our pride, and provoke our ambition; and even try to lead us to presume upon our faith, or to give it up; will do anything to seduce us from Christ and steal from Him our souls.

If he can keep the sinner from thinking about religion he is sure of his destruction; but if he will think, Satan will try to make him believe a lie; and if almost persuaded to be a Christian, he will plead for procrastination; and even after one believes in Christ, the evil one will try in every way to lead him astray; and when he has brought him into backsliding, he will try to make him believe that he never was a Christian, or that he has utterly fallen from grace, or that he has committed the unpardonable sin, and that there is no hope for him.

But the Holy Spirit, who knows the end from the beginning, would keep us from the very beginnings of evil, and would deliver us from all the wiles of the devil.

He knows, too, what is necessary to this end, and the means He uses are never more severe than are required for our deliverance. If His providence seems severe it is because severe measures alone will cure and save us. It may be necessary even to take us from the world, or, if not, to take the world from us. Just as we would take away from our children sharp tools which they had not learned to use and with which they would injure themselves; so He takes from us those things which would pierce our hearts; or, as we would keep them from going where they might receive harm, so He keeps us from our desires and plans and ambitions, which would bring us into evil or bring evil to us.

Loss of property or position or reputation, failures, humiliations, and defeats, are not the worst things that befall us, but often prove to be our best blessings in disguise. It is hard to give up and come down, but this may be the very means of a surer and safer exaltation. Very much of this mystery of providence shall be made clear as we go on in life and get a broader outlook over its course. What we know not now we shall know hereafter. That is truest comfort which deals with us in faithfulness, even when it is unpleasant to the Comforter and grievous to us. He is love even more in taking away than in giving, and we may learn to say trustfully, if not joyfully, "The Lord gave and the Lord hath taken away, blessed be the name of the Lord." If we fail to recognize the love of the Spirit in our afflictions, we shall fail not only of His comfort, but of our own peace and hope, and have no support when we need to realize His presence and to rest in Him.

James writes concerning afflictions: "Take, my brethren, the prophets, who have spoken in the name of the Lord, for an example of suffering, affliction, and patience. Behold, we call them blessed which endure. Ye have heard of the patience of Job and have seen the end of the Lord, how that the Lord is full of pity and merciful."

In the Epistle to the Hebrews, after the roll-call of the heroes of faith, among whom Abraham offered up Isaac in faith that God could, if need be, raise him even from the dead, to keep His covenant; and Moses, who chose rather to suffer affliction with the people of God than to enjoy the pleasures of sin for a season, and who endured as seeing Him who was invisible, there follows: "Ye have not resisted unto blood, striving against sin. And ye have forgotten the exhortation which reasoneth with you as sons. My son, regard not lightly the chastisement of the Lord, nor faint when thou art rebuked of Him; for whom the Lord loveth He chasteneth, and scourgeth every son whom He receiveth." "All chastening seemeth for the present to be not joyous, but grievous; yet afterward it yieldeth peaceable fruit unto them that are exercised thereby, even the fruit of righteousness."

THE SPIRIT A COMFORTER. 109

Here we see the patient and faithful mother-love of the Spirit in training the sons of God. And this agrees with what St. Paul says, in the precious and comforting eighth chapter of Romans, to which reference has already been made, where, after he speaks of the witness of the Spirit to our adoption as sons of God and to our freedom and joy and heirship, he immediately mentions suffering with Christ and like Him, that we may be glorified together; and then, as if some one had broken in with the question, "Why do you mention suffering so abruptly, if at all?" he replies, "I reckon that the sufferings of this present time are not worthy to be compared with the glory that shall be revealed to usward." Further on he speaks of the hope that, " the creature itself shall be delivered from the bondage of corruption into the liberty of the glory of the children of God."

Again, he writes to the Corinthians: "For our light affliction, which is for the moment, worketh for us more and more exceedingly an eternal weight of glory."

In the 119th Psalm, in which the psalmist gathers up all wisdom, he gives this as his experience: "Before I was afflicted I went away; but now have I kept Thy word. . . . . It is good for me that I have been afflicted, that I might learn Thy statutes. . . . . Thou in faithfulness hast afflicted me."

We can make no greater mistake than to refuse to see the hand and hear the voice of God in our afflictions. Failing in this we lose the help of the Comforter and become rebellious, hardening our hearts. The same sun and rain which mellow at one time, harden at another, according as the soil receives them. Instead of showing that He has gone far away and forgotten and forsaken us and is our enemy, they prove the very opposite: that He loves us, and is our true and faithful friend. By this means He would save us from some greater loss or evil, or prepare us for some greater blessing. The blessings He would have given us are more than we have received, and those He has prepared for us are more than we desire. He has a storehouse full of the missed and reserved blessings of the saints.

If we will go after and worship an idol to our debasement, He destroys it; or, if we will sleep in the midst of danger, He awakens and alarms us. And He awakens us sometimes with a crash that we may hear. When we come to love darkness and shut out the light, it is a mercy if He smashes in the blinds and windows. When a storm is brooding He startles us with His thunder. Whatever means He finds necessary to use will be blessed to us, if we see His hand in them. And it will be wise even to kiss the hand that holds the rod of reproof.

Nothing is sadder than to see the afflicted aggravate their afflictions by staying away from God, and seeking comfort from every other source, miserable comforters all; instead of going to the God of all comfort who alone can sustain and heal; and who has afflicted only that they might be made willing to accept His help. If we could but see it, the Spirit's ministry of affliction is, like His work in the conviction of sin, a marked evidence of His love. Instead of complaining, "Why should God permit me to be so afflicted?" we should rather say, "Why should He love me so?" Neither Christ nor the Spirit came to punish, but to save; and their discipline is in love.

The word chastisement, which expresses the nature of the affliction, means originally the bringing up or training of a child, and from that derives a secondary meaning of education, discipline, or chastisement. Its object is not penal, but disciplinary. Christians are in the school of the Spirit, preparing for a heavenly life.

In the case of the backslider and prodigal it is easy to see the great love that bears long with them, and follows them until they are brought to repentance. This is expressed in the exhortation, "Turn, O backsliding children," saith the Lord, "for I am married unto you,"—a spiritual union which knows no divorce.

The ultimate object of the captivity of the children of Israel was that they might forever be cured of idolatry; and none of them were brought back until it was certain that they would never again fall into that sin.

And even when affliction comes in the death of our dearest beloved, the Spirit is most our Comforter and loves us best. "There is no experience which comes to our homes which so affects and changes our lives as sickness; and should the sickness be unto death, a lesson has been learned which can never be forgotten. The glory of God never so fills our houses as when the angel of death is there, and the dear dust, which still retains the features of our beloved, awaits its burial in the sleeping-place. If we can realize that the Spirit has gone to God who gave it and hear Jesus say, 'I am the resurrection and the life,' we have learned the best lesson of life." *

We should be silent then, for God speaks. David did not murmur at such a time, but was dumb, for God did it. How gently the Spirit deals with us! How softly He whispers peace to our hearts! How He longs to make this a great blessing to us, revealing Christ and opening heaven as never before. And when the dear one goes home in peace, and the weary one enters into rest eternal,

---

* "Summer at Peace Cottage," p. 317.

and the sufferer has no more tears forever; when faith rejoices and triumphs in victory and the anchor holds within the veil; then do we also triumph in the same faith both for ourselves and our loved one and thank God, "who giveth us the victory through Jesus Christ our Lord." We do not now speak of cold submission to God,— that any philosopher can counsel; but we do far more, for we believe in Christ, we cast ourselves into the comforting arms, we weep on the heart whose every beat is love; we go and tell Jesus, and know that He doeth all things well. We do indeed submit; but it is a trustful, restful, joyful submission, which says in fullness of faith, "Not my will, but Thine be done."

We would not dare for a moment to have our own way. Even in the loss of our dearest treasures, the failure of our most cherished ambitions, the death of our best beloved, we would say, first of all, "Thy will be done."

That which is nearest to our hearts we would have in the hands of God to be guided by His wisdom and love. While his child was yet alive, David wept and fasted and prayed; but when the child died, and God had spoken, he arose and ate bread and went about his work.

There is greatest comfort in the assurance that "He who spared not His own Son, but delivered Him up for us all, will with Him also freely give us all things," and that, "Nothing shall separate us from the love of God, which is in Jesus Christ our Lord."

When we consider the Captain of our salvation, who was made perfect through sufferings, we do not wonder that afflictions are necessary for our sanctification.

We also learn to say, " Blessed be the God and Father of our Lord Jesus Christ, the Father of mercies and the God of all comfort, who comforteth us in all our afflictions, that we may be able to comfort them that are in any affliction with the comfort wherewith we ourselves are comforted of God. For as the sufferings of Christ abound in us, even so our comfort aboundeth through Christ."

If, therefore, we be comfortless it cannot be the fault of the Holy Comforter. He would ever say to us, " God rules, God knows, God loves"; and we may also say in holy confidence with Eli: "It is the Lord, let Him do what seemeth Him good "; or with Job, " Though He slay me, yet will I trust in Him "; or with the Shunamite, " It is well "; or, better, with Christ Himself, when He drank the bitter cup to its dregs in dark Gethsemane, " If it be possible, let this cup pass from me; nevertheless not my will but Thine be done."

We see also that our afflictions are intended to

make us workers together with the Spirit in comforting others. If we would be comforters we must first ourselves have wept. And as we were "created unto good works" by the Spirit, so we are to increase and abound more and more. We are to be brought into sympathy with Christ in all things, walking in the Spirit and working in the Spirit. Not only will he who has been comforted comfort others, but he who has been saved will seek to save others. Chastisement and discipline will make one more useful and faithful, abounding in good works. It is difficult to believe that a man, particularly a rich man, has faith in Christ unless he be liberal and active in spreading the Gospel. One cannot have much of the Holy Spirit dwelling in him, who is not in fullest sympathy with the work of missions. We are convicted and regenerated and sanctified for something more than our own salvation. We should be one with the Spirit in seeking the glory of Christ.

Christ, who is all and in all, should be in all our thoughts and plans; in our business and in all our living, as well as in our dying. We are to serve Him on earth, and thereby be prepared to adorn as well as to enjoy heaven. We are to engage in heavenly service as well as to partake of heavenly bliss, and for this we must be fully sanctified. Christians are called witnesses and confessors, and this often requires that they become, as the original implies, martyrs. They best save the life who lose it.

Among those whom the seer, in the vision of the Apocalypse, saw in white robes as peculiarly blessed, were those "who came out of great tribulation, and who washed their robes and made them white in the blood of the Lamb."

The diamond is the perfect gem, but that its utmost brilliancy may be brought out it must be ground until as many facets as possible shall reflect the light of the sun.

Mr. Philip says :* "Tell to yourself the kind and degree of sanctifying influence, which the Holy Spirit must put forth upon your heart and character, before you are 'meet to be a partaker of the inheritance of the saints in light.' Only consider how much He must do in you and for you even before your calling and election be sure to yourself. And now think, and think deeply, what He must do when you are dying, in order to fit you for *any kind* of an entrance into the everlasting kingdom of God, of holiness, of glory! What finishing touches He must give to the divine image, now so faint and imperfect in your soul. What ripeness He must produce, then, in all the fruits of holiness now so unripe. What

---

* "Love of the Spirit," chap. x.

a volume of holy fire He must throw into and around your spirit, to prepare you fully to meet God, to see the Lamb on His throne, to mingle with the general assembly of perfect saints, to sustain the blaze and weight and work of unveiled immortality."

We are complete in Christ, and the Holy Spirit has undertaken to make us complete in ourselves. Christ was touched with a feeling of our infirmities, and ministered unto us even to laying down His life for us; the Spirit " helpeth our infirmities " and abides our Comforter and Helper, in life and in death, sanctifying until He can present us holy and unblamable and unreprovable in His sight.

Counting fully all the cost of a Christian life: its self-denial and cross bearing, its mortification of the body, its separation from the world, its death to sin; all its trials and sufferings, who that has ever believed in Christ for the forgiveness of sin and the salvation of his soul, would exchange his portion for all that the world can give? Compared with the comfort of the Holy Spirit in the love of Christ, in the peace of God and in the hope of glory, all others are miserable comforters indeed.

Who does not rejoice as much that the Holy Spirit is his Sanctifier, as that Christ is his sanctification?

Who would have the will of God anything less than our sanctification, when the Spirit maketh intercession for the saints according to the will of God, whatever means He may use, until we shall be presented perfect in Christ Jesus?

Blessed be God, the Holy Spirit, the God of all comfort.

CHAPTER IX.

THE HOLY SPIRIT IN PRAYER.

THERE is no more encouraging promise than that of our Saviour, in which He assures us that our Heavenly Father is more willing to give the Holy Spirit to them that ask Him than earthly parents are to give good gifts to their children.

The gift of the Holy Spirit is the gift of gifts, all gifts in one. His is the coming of the King. He is God abiding in us, the Author of gifts and graces. And He was purchased for us at priceless cost and is given without measure to the Church.

Pentecost revealed the fullness and power and glory of His coming, the first-fruits and earnest of His work. And He is given freely to them that ask Him; and in answer to prayer, goes to those that ask Him not. We may not only come to God as the Hearer of prayer, and to His throne as to a throne of grace; but may say, "Our Father which art in Heaven," with the promise, "Ask and it shall be given you; seek and ye shall find; knock and it shall be opened unto you," having no limit except what is contained in the words, "Heavenly Father."

Better still, we may pray for the Holy Spirit, and this will put all prayers into one; for having the Holy Spirit we have the divine presence and power. He is a present divine Teacher, and Helper, and Comforter; dwelling ever in our hearts.

Our Saviour assured His disciples that whatsoever they should ask in His name He would do, that the Father might be glorified in the Son. The Spirit also glorifies the Father in the Son, and is given and comes and works in Jesus' name. Thus the love of the Father and the love of the Son and the love of the Spirit in the glorious plan of redemption, shine forth again in prayer, to hear which appears as one of the immutable and eternal characteristics of the divine government.

Everything that pertains to prayer is under the direction of the divine love, and especially that part which relates to the Holy Spirit.

This great privilege, purchased by the love of Christ, is enjoyed through the love of the Spirit. When His disciples asked Him, "Lord, teach us to pray," our Lord taught them the prayer commonly called "The Lord's Prayer."

But when He promised to send them the Comforter, He gave them the Inspirer and Teacher of Prayer, for an ever-present Helper, who would show them the way to the Father through the

Son and lead and keep them in it. Living as we now do under the dispensation of the Spirit, and having to do with Him in all our relations to the Godhead and dependent directly on Him for all spiritual blessings, what can be better for us than the promise and gift of the Spirit when we ask for Him?

Having this gift we pray in the Spirit. Praying in the Spirit, Jude says we build ourselves up in the faith and keep ourselves in the love of God. And St. Paul writes to the Ephesians, exhorting, "Praying always with all prayer and supplication in the Spirit."

All kinds and parts of prayer and at all seasons are to be in the Spirit, and there is no praying apart from the Spirit. There is as much need of praying in the Spirit as there is of praying in the name of Christ. We will not pray and know not how to pray, or what to pray for as we ought, or how even to plead Jesus' name except the Spirit moves and teaches and helps us. Praying in the Spirit is praying with the Spirit; co-operating with Him as He influences and directs us to pray; praying when He prays in and with us.

We are in the Spirit when we think and feel and love and act as He would have us, when we are willing and trusting and obedient, when He dwells in us and we have His communion.

Stephen, "full of the Holy Ghost," prayed,

"seeing the heavens opened." The colored man explained how we could be in the Spirit and the Spirit in us, by the illustration of the red-hot poker, " The fire was in the poker when the poker was in the fire."

Praying for the Spirit is praying for all that His presence and work implies, for convicting power, for regenerating power, for gracious power, and these are illustrated by pentecostal power. Following this is illuminating and sanctifying power, the power of an endless life. When this power is present the Church is endued also with power from on high, and sinners cry out to know what they must do to be saved; blessings are poured out more than there is room to receive. Its influence is like showers of refreshing from the presence of the Lord. Without this gift there could be no Church.

Our Saviour's promise to His disciples to be in their midst when two or three are gathered together in His name has in it the presence and potency of the Holy Spirit at the command of the Church. And it is also in this connection that He gives the Church the keys by which heaven is opened and shut. Heaven is opened by prayer. It is in the prayer-meeting that the Church is filled with the Holy Ghost, and they who love the place of prayer will be in the Spirit.

Praying in the Spirit, one has power with God

and with men; the Spirit ministers to him, and at his request, and his prayer belts the globe. Prayer moves the power that moves the world.

But there is something more and even better for us than praying for and praying in the Spirit, blessed as are these privileges.

We may pray *to* the Spirit.

Prayer may be offered directly to Him as well as to the Father and to the Son, and all the more now that we are under the dispensation of the Spirit. Praying to the Spirit, we shall more easily recognize His presence and indwelling, and, realizing this with His personal love for us, we have not only the greatest privilege, but also greatest joy in the communion of the Holy Spirit.

Some one has said: "In prayer we talk with God, and in the Word God talks with us." Praying to the Spirit will be like conversing with a personal and present friend and helper. He will indeed be a very present help in trouble.

This enlarges our idea of prayer by as much as it increases its privilege and blessing, adding a third person to its scope. Until we pray to the Spirit we shall fail to realize His divinity as we might. That we may pray for Him and in Him and to Him greatly enriches prayer and doubly assures of what we ask.

Here, then, is a wide scope for the practical development of Christian doctrine, as well as a rich field for the development of religious experience. The Church does not yet know the fullness of its creed, " I believe in the Holy Ghost," and has not yet begun to learn to pray to Him. Very seldom in the rituals of the Church do we find any direct personal petitions to the Holy Spirit, while everywhere we find petitions for Him.

Here, also, the Spirit's benevolence and His absorption in the glory of Christ appear in that, while we must pray in the name of Christ and in the Spirit, He does not speak of His own love as manifest in what He does; but delights to magnify Christ's love in what He suffered and the Father's love in what He gave for us.

In connection with prayer to the Holy Spirit, we see the genius of poetry by which the poet, with his spiritual insight, utters spiritual truths not found in formulas of doctrine and duty. In our hymnology we pray to, as well as praise, the Holy Spirit, directly and naturally, as is witnessed by the fact that in the most popular collection of spiritual songs, out of thirty hymns under the head of the Holy Spirit, twenty-three are direct petitions to the Spirit.

These will be recognized at once as the most precious of our hymns, showing how practically we have learned more than we have realized of this precious privilege and truth of prayer to the

Spirit. The opening lines of a few of these hymns show this peculiarity of hymnology :

> " Come, Holy Spirit, come."
> " Come, Holy Spirit, Heavenly Dove."
> " Come, Creator, Spirit, blest."
> " Eternal Spirit, we confess."
> " Blest Comforter Divine."
> " Holy Ghost, the Infinite."
> " O Spirit of the Living God."
> " Gracious Spirit, love Divine."

Such direct address to the Spirit will not only increase the preciousness and power of prayer, but will add greatly to our knowledge of and faith in the Spirit Himself.

We shall never again be content to pray simply for the Spirit—great as is that privilege—now that we know the other and still greater privilege; but shall feel the same liberty in coming to Him that we do in coming to the Father and to the Son, and all the more boldly shall we come to Him also in Jesus' name. We shall also the more joyfully welcome Him when He graciously comes to us, and shall give Him a sanctuary in our hearts.

We cannot realize too strongly not only the importance of prayer, but also its very necessity to any spiritual life and growth. It holds a first place in the plan of God for saving sinners and sanctifying the saints.

> "Prayer was appointed to convey
> The blessings God designs to give."

Only by prayer do we reach the throne of grace and make known our wants to God. Unless some one prays for the impenitent, the way is not open for the Spirit to go to him according to the honorable condition of divine reconciliation. Acceptable prayer must be in the name of Christ, to be also in the Spirit. And such prayer is the substance of all worship. In prayer we first lisp in spiritual speech; we confess our sins and cry out for mercy; we ask for daily bread, and pour out to God our adoration and praise and thanksgiving, and commune in rapt devotion and exalted communion. Prayer is like the simple cry of an infant for light and food and mother-love, and the relation of parent and child is not more natural than the Fatherhood of God and the Brotherhood of the Son and the Motherhood of the Spirit. As asking is the way of getting others to do for us what we need, so prayer is the natural expression of our filial relation to God.

And while it has in it childlike simplicity and naturalness, it also engages all one's powers, and is the highest and most glorious activity of the human spirit. Well has prayer been called "the instinct of humanity."

Knowledge of God and growth in grace as

well as divine help come through prayer. A Christian cannot live a spiritual life without it. It is no exaggeration to say that

> " Prayer is the Christian's vital breath,
> The Christian's native air."

And as parents must teach their children how to ask and what to ask for, and train them in the doing of it, so the children of God need to be taught and trained by the Spirit in prayer.

And they who are full of the Holy Spirit become mighty in prayer and prevail with God.

The more we magnify prayer the greater appears the privilege of praying to the Spirit; and no one will think of praying except in the Spirit.

Mr. Philip says:* "We must no more allow ourselves to forget the Spirit when we open our Bible, or enter the sanctuary, or engage in prayer than we overlook the Father and the Son. We are to be as afraid of grieving Him as of dishonoring them; for as we profess to ascribe equal and everlasting glory to Father, Son, and Spirit, we ought to pay them equal attention."

Praying to the Spirit is not only more direct than praying for the Spirit, but one thus realizes as in no other way His presence, and takes hold more strongly on His power; and while he worships Him directly, he asks more boldly and freely

---

* " Love of the Spirit," chap. viii.

His help and grace, and feels more assured of His love.

There is a divine philosophy in prayer in harmony with the human environment by which it develops the highest that is in man through the laws of mind and spirit with which he was created. Thus prayer has a more intimate connection with his sanctification by the Spirit than any other instrumentality.

No one can come to God in any part of prayer without spiritual uplift and blessing. Not only does God hear and answer prayer, but we by prayer are fitted to receive the answer to the very prayer we offer. The reflex influence of prayer is often its greatest blessing. We are transformed into the image of Him to whom we pray in all true worship.

When one draws near to God in prayer he realizes the divine presence as not at other times, and opens his heart as a sanctuary, which for the time becomes a Bethel, a house of God—a ladder is let down from heaven on which angels ascend and descend. He bares his head and stands on holy ground, for he sees God face to face. And as he looks upon His face of insufferable splendor, the divine being and perfections shine forth with an effulgence which reveals more and more the glory of God, until his eyes are blinded by the very brightness of the light.

The Spirit takes the things of Christ and shows them unto him, and sheds abroad the love of Christ in his heart, until he is rapt with Him who is altogether lovely, and filled with wonder, love, and praise. He breaks forth in adoration, ascribing to God His honors and perfections. "Hallowed be Thy name," he prays; and such is seen to be the glory of His sovereignty that he continues, "Thy kingdom come; Thy will be done in earth as it is in heaven."

Another important effect of prayer is that when one draws near to God he sees more vividly by comparison his own sinfulness; and as the Spirit reveals the divine holiness, the sinner is convicted of sin, and will confess it and repent of it in deepest humiliation. Prayer will teach him his need of pardon and grace, and lead him to cry for mercy.

When the Spirit renews the heart and witnesses of pardon and justification and adoption, it sings a doxology of praise and thanksgiving. Then, made bold by its success, it goes on more freely, and becomes a suppliant, presenting freely and boldly, not only personal petitions in the name of Christ, but also pleads for others, becoming in turn an intercessor.

Thus every time one engages in prayer he feels the sanctifying touch of the Holy Spirit upon him, and prayer becomes the chief means of sanctification. And we are commanded to pray without ceasing, which means that we are to sanctify the Holy Spirit in our hearts, so that we can at any time withdraw into the chamber of our consciousness, and meet Him there and hold communion with Him. And having the Spirit with us in consciousness, we shall not only be kept from sinning, but shall be strong in His help.

The presence of a great and good man would keep one from profanity and intemperance and other sins; much more will the presence of the Holy Spirit, who mightily helpeth our infirmities, keep us from falling.

But we are yet far from seeing all of the love of the Spirit in prayer. Having noticed its blessed privilege and its sanctifying influence, we do not wonder that the Spirit, in His love for us, would have us ever in a prayerful frame and grow into the fullest measure of this grace. We may not only pray for the Spirit and in the Spirit and to the Spirit; but, what is equally blessed, He moves us to pray, and would teach us how to pray and pray with us, suggesting prayer to us, interceding with us to pray in time of need; and when we know not what to pray for as we ought, "He maketh intercession for us with groanings which cannot be uttered." Such is His love for us that He makes our infirmities His own and bears our burdens with us. And the love of the

Godhead is equally manifested in the privilege and blessing of prayer; for as it was in accordance with the divine plan from all eternity to hear prayer, so prayer was presupposed in the plan and work of redemption as the chief means through which the love of the Father in giving Christ, and of Christ in dying for our salvation, and of the Spirit in applying His redemption, should be known and received by us; so that the prayer of faith is the channel of blessing.

Mr. Philip sets this forth with such richness and clearness that I quote him at length.*

"It is just as true that the Spirit ever liveth to help our infirmities by suggesting prayer, as that the Saviour ever liveth to intercede for the prayerful. Indeed the respective offices of the Father, Son, and Spirit, in reference to prayer, seem to sustain each other. The Father's readiness to hear seems to be as much as the Spirit's reason for helping our infirmities and the Son's reason for pleading His own merits on our behalf, as their joint intercession is the Father's reason for answering prayer. He answers it because the Spirit suggests it and the Son presents it, and they promote it thus because He delights to hear it." .... Again, "Christ will no more put heartless prayers into His censer than God will answer

---

* "Love of the Spirit," chap. vii.

Christless prayer. . . . . Whosoever will not pray in the name of Jesus, the Father will not answer him, and whosoever will not yield to the strivings of the Spirit, the Son will not own him."

Thus the way to God in prayer is all prepared in love, and no one has any excuse for not praying, and for this reason all are commanded to pray, and not to pray is a chief sin. And the excuse that one has not the Spirit is the most insincere of all. One may go to the Spirit as freely as to his Bible. And no one is long without the strivings of the Spirit; even from youth to old age He pleads and waits and would be gracious.

Long ago would He have left the sinner had He not been divine love. The trouble is, the sinner has already more striving of the Spirit than He likes, than is agreeable with His sin and worldliness; and must either turn from his sin or shut the door on the Spirit. He stops his ear to His entreaties and grieves and provokes and quenches and even blasphemes Him, and sins before Him and sins against Him.

And yet, "God is more willing to give the Holy Spirit to them that ask Him than earthly parents are to give good gifts to their children," and the Holy Spirit is just as willing to come.

CHAPTER X.

THE INTERCESSION OF THE SPIRIT.

WHEN one first begins to pray there is a joy in the Holy Spirit which he never knew before; and there is joy with the saints and the angels of God when it can be said of a sinner, " Behold, he prayeth." And one who has experienced this knows that joy and peace will be found again at the throne of grace, and only there, however far he may have wandered from God.

All the Spirit's dealings with the backslider are to bring him back again to his closet.

And the only safety for any Christian is in a habit of prayer, which implies constant communion with the Spirit.

Besides this, we are warned to " watch unto prayer," and to " watch and pray lest we enter into temptation." And in His great love, unwearied, the Spirit watches with us, and while we sleep watches over and for us. So that when we feel His awakening touch we should arouse ourselves at once and arm for some conflict, or be ready for duty, or it may be to receive a much needed blessing.

Mr. Philip puts it in this way :* "There is, depend upon it, a strong needs-be whenever the Holy Spirit bears in upon the mind the conviction that there must be more prayer than usual. He foresees some imminent or real danger to our principles, our character, or our peace, whenever He stirs us to cry mightily to God. This is the signal He gives to warn us of approaching trials, of something about to happen which we are not prepared for by our ordinary devotions. Either trouble is coming, which we are not fit to sustain with our present strength, or temptations are coming which we are not able to overcome by it; either our spiritual affairs are on the eve of some turn, or Satan has taken measures to 'sift us as wheat,' and therefore we must fail unless our Intercessor in heaven pray for us. The Spirit foresees and forewarns and intercedes that Christ may intercede for us. . . . . Oh, what falls and shipwrecks and apostasies and backslidings might have been prevented had all those who are thus challenged and charged, when they began to decline from their first love, been obedient to the heavenly vision."

When our Lord was about to enter on any great crisis of His ministry, such as the choosing of His disciples, or the refusing of earthly king-

---

* "Love of the Spirit," chap. vii.

dom, or the laying down of His life, He spent all night in prayer.

We shall be blessed when we endure temptation, but this blessedness will not be ours without the help of the Holy Spirit. Only in His strength shall we grow strong. And we should go on from strength to strength, and growth in and through prayer will be the best growth in grace. This will increase access to grace and grasp all blessing.

The Spirit will not leave us satisfied with forgiveness of sin and union with Christ; He would have us perfect in Christ Jesus. We are to inherit all the promises, and in order to this He must "bring them to our remembrance and build them up in our prayers." He gives us the arguments we make before the throne, and furnishes our pleas in prayer, and teaches us what is according to the will of God.

He awakens the hunger and thirst after righteousness we feel. It is as important that we have a sense of our privileges and a holy ambition after likeness to Christ and witness for heaven as that we be kept in temptation. And what light and grace we need to fit us "to see as we are seen and to know as we are known"; to be "at home in Heaven." And prayer in the Spirit is the nearest earth gets to heaven. We open as well as enter heaven with prayer.

St. Paul hints at depths of ignorance, both of ourselves and of God, when he says, "We know not what we should pray for as we ought." Our sinful nature, our weakness, our easily besetting sins, our lack of wisdom, the power of the evil one, are all included in this ignorance concerning our praying. But he adds, and here is our help and victory, "The Spirit helpeth our infirmities." And what help can compare with His help. When we are weak and go to Him, then are we strong; His help is divine help and wisdom and strength; help that never leaves nor forsakes; help that never fails. He taketh our infirmities upon Himself, and is so one with us, that "He maketh intercession for us with groanings that cannot be uttered." This reveals a personal love that cannot be measured or exhausted. His very spirit agonizes over and for and with us in our spiritual infirmities; and His grief over us is because we do not or will not allow Him to deliver us, and bestow the fullness of the peace and liberty of Christ, and lead us into the fullness of blessing. How many blessings we have lost; even so many are yet in store for us if we will have them. His is the spirit of a pitying Helper, and not of a condemning Judge. And such a time is a spiritual crisis, when we are in imminent danger of being overcome of evil or of losing a most needed blessing. To grieve the

Spirit at such a time is fearful beyond expression.

We may not realize it, but the angels do, and wait with bated breath when we are in danger of refusing the intercession of the Holy Spirit. When He moves us to prayer, it is the drawing of our wisest and best Friend in His perfect knowledge and most faithful love.

Sometimes there is such urgency in it that there is time only to ejaculate a cry for help, like that of sinking Peter, "Lord, save! I perish!"

But some one may ask, "If these things be so; if the Spirit so loves to help us in prayer, why is it that our prayers so often go unanswered?" It is true indeed that many prayers, which we think were offered in the Spirit, are not yet answered. It is also possible that we may be deceived about the spirit of our prayers, or that the best time for their answer has not yet come. The smoke of the incense of these prayers of the saints, if they were moved by the Spirit, has come before God, and in good time He will pour out answers of blessing.

In the chapter on Prayer, in "The Law of Love," President Mark Hopkins says: * "Asking is not simply desire expressed, but paramount desire. There must be a desire for the thing asked greater than for anything else that would

---

* "Law of Love," p. 315.

be incompatible with it. . . . . . Prayer is an act of choice. . . . . Prayer is more than desire, more than sincere desire. It is paramount desire offered to God with a filial spirit."

We may greatly desire what we know is good, and ask for it, when at the same time we desire something else, and choose and seek that. The head may pray for one thing and the heart for another. We may assent to and yield to the Spirit's intercession in part, and not trust Him fully so as to put ourselves unreservedly under His guidance. We ask according to our own wills, and not according to the will of God. God will be sought and found only with the whole heart, and cannot accept less. We may not make conditions in our prayers. Oftener than we know we deceive ourselves even in our prayers.

And we may not ask for, nor will the Spirit help us to get, what we can obtain for ourselves. There is no need that He should assist us, nor that we should plead the name of Christ for what we can get in our own name. The Spirit helps our weakness, and not our strength. And His best help is given when He helps us to help ourselves. This is wisest aid. He works in us and through us, when anything can be done in this way, and not independent of us. He can and will work superhuman and miraculous works for us when they become necessary. He intercedes

THE INTERCESSION OF THE SPIRIT. 139

with us and teaches us how to pray, and what to pray for, and moves us mightily and strengthens us with all grace, and even groans within us in His desire to help us; but He does not finally choose for us: that is our own responsible and sovereign act. Everything that the most loving and powerful and wisest friend can do for us He does for us, and stops not short of our final choice. It can never be the Spirit's fault if our prayers are unanswered.

"When God inclines the heart to pray,
He has an ear to hear."

And the Spirit's intercessions are according to the will of God.

St. James says: "Ye ask and receive not because ye ask amiss, that ye may spend it on your sins."

No wise parent will give his son money to spend in sin, but he will spend his money for him until he learns to use it wisely for himself.

God will give us as much as we can use and as fast as we can use it. Many unanswered prayers are for what we can get ourselves by common means. Many are unanswered for want of cooperation in that part we can answer ourselves. Many are lazy prayers which we care too little about to follow up; many selfish that we may get blessings without effort; many thoughtless, which we would not have answered if we knew their cost, and the answer is withheld in mercy; and many are unanswered because we do not ask in whole-hearted sincerity. We pray,

> "Nearer, my God, to Thee,
> Nearer to Thee,
> E'en though it be a cross
> That raiseth me,"

when we would be unwilling to take up the cross, which would have to be laid upon us to bring us nearer. And it may be that our prayers are Christless prayers, not offered in penitence for sin and with realization of our need of mercy and help, and therefore not according to the promise, asking blessings upon our sin; prayers for escape from the penalty of sin, and not for freedom from sin itself.

Then again our prayers may lack that filial trust which becomes the sons of God. We have not faith in the Spirit's guidance, which is the same as lack of faith in Christ. Faith trusts all and obeys. There is need of resignation and submission in prayer as in no other act.

We are asking of God as suppliants and children, and not dictating to Him how or when our prayers shall be answered. Nor do we ask in our own name, nor for any merit in us, but as sinners and in Christ's name. The prayer of prayers is this: "Not my will, but Thine be done"; and as our urgency increases and we draw nearer God, the better will we be satisfied with this one petition. We would not dare to dictate or press our dearest desire, and say, "My will, not Thine be done"; but would always say, "It is the Lord; let Him do what seemeth Him good."

President Mark Hopkins related an incident of a fond mother, who went away and prayed when her boy of three years lay dying, having been given up of the physicians: "Not Thy will, but *mine* be done. Give me the life of my boy." And the boy grew up to be a murderer, and died on the gallows.

We do well to ask the Spirit to teach us how to pray over our unanswered prayers, or to help us to wait patiently God's time to answer them.

But for the love of the Spirit in prayer, we would make sad work even of our prayers; with His intercession we may "come boldly to the throne of grace, that we may obtain mercy and find grace to help in our time of need."

There is still another phase of prayer which deserves more than a passing notice.

In prayer, we become unselfish like the Spirit, pleading the glory of God; which is also the highest good of all His creatures; for glorifying Him as his chief end, one enjoys Him forever, is blessed evermore. Since prayer is the channel of the Divine blessing, we become ourselves intercessors, with Christ and the Spirit, for others. As our heart's adoration and love go out to God in gratitude and praise, we pray, "Thy will be done." And in the proportion that we love our friends and our fellow-men, and have felt the grace of God, do we want them to know and love our Saviour and to receive the gracious influences of the Spirit. We press them upon the Spirit's attention and plead with Him in Jesus' name to go to them as He once came to us. We enter into fullest sympathy with the Spirit in seeking the glory of Christ, praying that He may see of the travail of His soul for a lost world. We labor and pray, devotedly and continually, for the upbuilding of His Church, the spread of the Gospel, and the work of missions. We would have the heathen become His inheritance and the uttermost parts of the earth His possession.

Every one, full of the Spirit, is full of zeal for the salvation of sinners and prays unceasingly, "Thy kingdom and Thy will be done in earth as it is in heaven." In answer to such prayer the Holy Spirit may go and will go to sinners, even to the chief of sinners, and to the abodes of sin and death, and offer salvation through Christ full and free. Our prayers may belt the world with more than electric speed.

When our friends will not pray for themselves,

who can tell what dangers they escape, and what blessings they receive when we pray for them at the intercession of the Spirit? Little does the sinner realize how much he owes to the prayers of his friends, and often he is forced to say, in connection with the Spirit's influence in some to him otherwise inexplicable providence, "Some one has been praying for me."

As we may not resist the Spirit's strivings with us to pray for ourselves, so we may not refuse to pray for others when He moves us, for thus we answer their cry for help. It may be spiritual life to them. There is through the Spirit a direct connection between our prayers and the salvation of sinners, and He loves to help us pray for them more than we love to pray.

Joel in his prophecy, as Peter in its fulfilment, connects the promise of God to " pour out of His Spirit upon all flesh," with the other promise that, " Whosoever shall call on the name of the Lord shall be saved." Pentecost was the answer to prayer; and this is always the Spirit's method of working.

Revivals of religion are the outpouring of the Spirit in answer to prayer, and are revivals of prayer in the Spirit; and so long as the prayer continues, so long the shower of refreshing will be poured out from the opened windows of heaven. Always to the end of the world, " to the consummation of the age," Christ will be with His Church through the Spirit, ever living to intercede for all who yield to the spirit's strivings to call upon His name.

Mr. Philip beautifully says:* "Yielding to the Spirit's intercession *with* us, secures Christ's intercession *for* us; Christ will put no prayer into His censer of much incense, which has not been put into our hearts by the Holy Spirit. And, on the other hand, it is just as true that Christ will not exclude from His golden censer any prayer which the Holy Spirit excites. It may not be answered at once, but it is sure to be presented, accepted, and remembered. It is as truly *filed* at the throne of God as it was felt by the heart or breathed by the lips."

The prayerless man must be very ignorant of experimental theology and of Christian life. The spirituality of an individual, as of a church, will be measured by his prayer in the Spirit.

Unless one has "a still hour," a "sweet hour of prayer," he has not progressed very far in heavenly citizenship.

It will not be uncharitable, in view of what we have learned of the love of the Spirit in prayer; of His burning desire to bring us to Christ and to sanctify us through prayer; of His grace to

---

* "Love of the Spirit," chap. vii.

help all our infirmities; and of the necessity of prayer in the Spirit to secure the intercession of Christ and the answer of the Father, if we say that the prayerless man must remain a Godless man and a Christless man and a Spiritless man. He abides in the sin and shame and condemnation of the carnal nature, and cannot see the kingdom of God except he be born of the Spirit of prayer. If for the Christian to cease praying be spiritual decline, never to pray is never to have entered into the life of God, is to live in an abiding state of spiritual death.

Christ was so touched with a feeling of our infirmities that He ministered to us even to the laying down of His life for us. With the same love, and with all divine power and grace, the Spirit comes to abide with us, to work in us and with us, to help our infirmities. Helpless and hopeless, as well as heartless, must he be who will not welcome and trust the Spirit of love.

As the high-priest wore upon his breast a breast-plate graven with the names of the twelve tribes of the children of Israel, and upon his shoulders stones graven also with their names, so Christ with every beat of His heart bears His own in love before the Father, and upholds them continually with His strength. Their names are graven upon His palms, where they are ever before His eyes. Even so with the same divine love and the same divine strength the Spirit abides with the disciples of Christ, and would keep them ever united to Him by His continual intercession with them, that He may present them at last without fault and blameless among the redeemed and glorified throng before the throne of God in heaven.

CHAPTER XI.

PROBATION OF THE HOLY SPIRIT.

THERE is no passage of the Scriptures which brings out more clearly the intimate relation of the Holy Spirit to Christ, and His co-operation with Christ in the work of redemption, and the absolute necessity of the spirit's help in making salvation effectual to the sinner, than that in which our Saviour rebukes the Scribes for their blasphemy in calling the spirit in Him that of Satan, and His work the work of Satan. He speaks here with strong affirmation and with divine authority: " Verily, I say unto you, all sins shall be forgiven unto the sons of men, and blasphemies wherewith soever they shall blaspheme; but he that shall blaspheme against the Holy Ghost hath never forgiveness, but is in danger of eternal damnation." The revision renders the last clause, " But is guilty of an eternal sin."

Note the strong words which the merciful Saviour here uses: " all sins," " wherewith soever," " never forgiveness," and " eternal sin."

The forgiveness of sin, a Divine prerogative, is connected directly with one's treatment of the Holy Spirit, and one may commit against Him a sin which hath never forgiveness eternally. Here is the crisis of such a sinner for eternity. To call the Holy Spirit of Christ an unclean spirit, and His work the work of the devil, the great arch-enemy of Christ, whom He utterly and infinitely abhors, and whose works He came to destroy, and whom He judges and punishes with everlasting vengeance, is the height of blasphemous sin. Not to give the Holy Spirit the honor due to Him; not to receive Him and believe Him and obey Him, is heinous sin in the sight of the Father and the Son who sent Him into the world. And to sin against Him is to sin against Father and Son as well as the Holy Spirit.

The Holy Spirit is most keenly sensitive to sin; not so sensitive is the photographer's plate to the sun, or the needle to the magnet. He is holy, and sin is Satanic; He is pure, and sin is vile; He is light, and sin is darkness; He is life, and sin is death. One is the destroyer of the other, and where sin is He must depart. He is holy in eternal being, nature, will, truth, and work; and dwells in holy heaven, the abode of holy and sanctified spirits. Sin must eternally be shut out of heaven, or it is defiled so as to be unfit for His dwelling-place. It must be shut up in hell, or it will spread over and corrupt the universe. For sin to enter heaven would be calamity unutterable, disaster irretrievable, anarchy universal. There is no other alternative for sin except death, its own wages.

A little child was troubled about the doom of a murderer, whose awful crime excited the horror of the community, and asked her mother again and again what God would do with him. The mother had told her child of heaven, but not of hell, and did not wish her to know anything about the latter place, and put her off with unsatisfactory answers, bidding her to wait for the solution of such questions until she was older. But the child could not so easily put aside the question, now that it was raised; and worked out the problem alone, and said to her mother: "God and I cannot let that murderer into heaven, for he would kill some one there. We will make a place outside of heaven, and shut him up there." This is the logic of holiness which cannot be refuted.

To sin before the Holy Spirit is most offensive; to sin against Him is most insulting; to call Him a sinner and a devil is blasphemy unpardonable. To neglect, to grieve, to deny, to provoke Him calls for holy vengeance.

The fearfulness of sin against the Holy Spirit

cannot be too deeply impressed. In any degree it is guilt deserving the penalty of the holy law, and has forgiveness only through the sacrifice of Christ; and there is a sin against Him which hath never forgiveness, but is an eternal sin, deserving eternal damnation.

The relation of the Holy Spirit to sin and of sin to the Holy Spirit has not enough been thought of, either by the Church or the world. God alone can reveal the exceeding sinfulness of sin, who alone knows its nature and vileness, and its evil and deadly results. It is sin against God the Father, God the Son, and God the Holy Ghost; against His eternal being and character; against His law and love and grace; against His creatures and His universe, its order and harmony and peace and blessing. It is disobedience, rebellion, and destruction; becoming worse and worse as time goes on; and sinners by their very sinfulness are less able to understand and realize its evil to them and to others.

There is one phase of this subject which is of unspeakable importance to man, which has scarcely been noticed, if written upon at all: that of the Spirit's relation to man's probation. A probation is a time of trial; the time of opportunity for a change, when alternatives of choice are open.

Joshua called the Israelites before him and said, "Choose ye this day whom ye will serve," whether the idol gods or Jehovah. Their probation of choice was for that day, and the alternatives were blessing and cursing, life and death. The choice was decisive, once for all, of the life service.

There is a supreme choice which is one's character, which is made according to the nature of the man, and is either carnal or spiritual; and this choice underlies and determines all acts of the will, and sets the current of being and life for or against God.

On the top of the Rocky Mountains is a watershed, where rain-drops from the same shower separate: some to go to the Atlantic and others to the Pacific, continent-wide apart at last. Such is a character-making and destiny-determining choice made in time and for eternity.

When now we consider that man is a sinner, by nature carnally-minded, which is death; that his being and life are of God and continually upheld by His power; that time is God's; that sin is ever under condemnation and deserves immediate death; and that the wrath of God is just as great against sin now as it will be at death, and in the judgment of the great day; that sin in man is as evil as it is in Satan and his fallen hosts,—to have given us the alternative of life instead of death which we deserve; the privilege of choosing again through the power of the Holy

Spirit and in the name of Christ, is an unspeakable blessing supremely and eternally precious; and shows how the long-suffering of God alone is our salvation.

Right here arises a momentous question, how long will this probation last? Any probation, even a single choice, would be a blessed privilege. A debtor would consider the extension of time for the payment of his debt a favor, and a reprieve from the execution of a death sentence would be the last hope of the doomed prisoner. Surely no rational man would refuse to embrace the first chance for pardon of sin, and put off to the very last his choice of life, and sin against the mercy of God as long as possible!

If an inhabitant of another planet, where sin and death were unknown, should visit the earth, he would be astonished first of all to find sin here; and still more to find that sin was not visited with immediate death; and then, if possible, he would be still more astonished, even amazed beyond measure, to learn that, after all God the Father and the Son and the Holy Spirit had done to save sinners, every sinner did not immediately and with all his heart embrace the offer of salvation, and think of and care for nothing else until he was assured of forgiveness and peace with God.

The whole trend of the Scriptures favors the

view that death ends probation; and that after death comes the judgment; yet there are those who think they find some hope that there is a probation, at least for a part of the race, after death; and others who argue that the boundless mercy of God will save all, or will continue probation beyond the grave until the general judgment, or if needs be through eternity.

It would seem at first thought a blessed thing if this larger hope were true, even if there were eternal hope.

But our final appeal must be to the Word of God; and here the answer will be given, not so certain by quoting detached passages of Scripture on either side, as by the teaching of the Scriptures concerning the relation of the Holy Spirit to man's probation; for his salvation depends entirely upon what the Holy Spirit can and will do in the matter and is altogether in His hands.

Probation here or hereafter is of the Holy Spirit.

Man was banished from Paradise by his sin, and cannot return except God remove the cherubim and flaming sword which guard the tree of life. Sin must be forgiven and cleansed, and God alone can forgive sin; and how He will forgive He alone can tell. There is no salvation here or hereafter outside the covenants of redemption and grace.

According to these God, in His love for the perishing world, gave His only-begotten Son, that the world should have eternal life through believing in Him and perish not. And there is no other way revealed by which to come to the Father; "none other name under heaven, given among men, whereby we must *be* saved." The Son of God Himself became his Redeemer, the only Substitute and Intercessor for sinful man.

But, as we have seen, the love of the Father was all in vain for him, and the sacrifice of Christ availed him not so long as man refused to come to the Father through the Son for life. There was further needed the love and work of the Holy Spirit to lead him to accept the covenant of grace, ever so freely offered. Unless the Spirit had undertaken to make effectual the redemption purchased by Christ, all were lost in the very sight of the cross.

The whole plan of redemption was of the mercy of God; and was formed outside of man and apart from the holy law; yet fulfilling the righteousness of the law. This wonderful redemption—involving the gift of the Father, the sacrifice of Christ, and the sanctification of the Spirit—was wholly of grace, in its inception, its offer and its application. The covenant of grace was in the hands of the Holy Spirit for ratification; and its final condition was His work of love with the sinner.

He sustained Christ in all His humiliation and suffering; and now, because of His sacrifice, will justify all who believe in Him.

The whole work of redemption, the interests of the Father and the Son in the world, all their relations of love and grace toward sinners, are in the hands of the Holy Spirit, and are now under His administration of the kingdom of heaven; and His authority shall continue until the day of Jesus Christ, when the work of redemption shall be closed up forever. Pentecost ushered in His personal administration: manifesting its power and grace and glory. He who inspired the Word must give it power in the hearts of men. He filled the apostles when laying the foundations of the Church. His is the work of convicting the world of sin. But for His convicting love and faithfulness no sinner would know or feel his sinfulness, so as to repent of it, and his need of the intercession of Jesus Christ.

But for His help no one would be persuaded or enabled to come to Christ for salvation. "Except a man be born of the Spirit he cannot enter into the kingdom of God." Regeneration is wholly His work here, and in the possibility of the hereafter. Every saved sinner must be washed, and justified and sanctified, in the name of the Lord

Jesus and by the Spirit of God; must be made "a new creature in Christ Jesus." And after regeneration, he must be "kept from falling," and made complete, sanctified fully and fitted for glory by the work of the Holy Spirit.

There is not a moment from the beginning to the end of his redemption in which he is not dependent on the love and work of the Spirit. The Spirit must teach him how to pray, and pray with him, and help him in his infirmities through all his sanctification. And we may not forget that He continues to be the same *Holy* Spirit all the time He is dwelling with us and dealing with our sinfulness and unbelief; and that all His work is in Divine love: done for nothing in us and while we are sinful and evil.

It is plain that we are shut up to the Spirit's help in all our salvation. He may help when He pleases and while He pleases and as He pleases; and would help all. Whenever and wherever He comes to help, salvation is not only possible, but assured for all who trust in Christ. And we are exhorted to "seek the Lord while He may be found, and to call on Him while He is near."

When He helps, "He maketh intercession for us according to the will of God," and Christ also intercedes for us and the Spirit presents our petitions.

And "that which is born of the flesh is flesh,"

remains flesh, and "that which is born of the Spirit is spirit." The carnal heart cannot, will not change itself, nor of itself repent and accept Christ, be its probation longer or shorter.

If, therefore, the Holy Spirit does not come to a sinner at all, there is never any salvation for him forever; or if He leaves him, not to return, there can never be any salvation for him; and when He finally departs, his probation is thereby forever ended—his doom is sealed. That last sin, be it great or small, which wears out the patience of the Spirit of God and grieves Him to depart; at which He finally leaves a sinner to himself, is necessarily an eternal sin. It abides sin eternally and decides eternity.

There will be no more strivings of the Spirit; no more offers of forgiveness; no more possibility of regeneration; no more sanctifying grace; no more prayer in the Spirit. The sinner is not only spiritually dead, but dead and buried, helpless and hopeless forever. He has said to the Holy Spirit, depart; and Christ on the throne will say to him, depart everlastingly. Probation for time and eternity ends whenever the Spirit's love and grace are finally accepted or rejected.

The probation of Christians ends when they believe in Christ, and at the time of their regeneration—ends in salvation. They are henceforth in Christ, united to Him, and sons of God, which is eternal life. "He that believeth on the Son hath eternal life."

In the same sense the probation of unbelievers ends when the Spirit finally leaves them to themselves, at the crisis of choice which rejects His help; it may be in youth, or in middle life, or at old age. They need not wait until death to end their probation. With all it is in the body and therefore in this world being decided by the " deeds done in the body," according to which judgment is rendered. The last possible hope will be in dying light and dying grace; and we would not limit the almighty power and infinite love of the Spirit in this last extremity; for the blood of Christ is adequate to the cleansing from all sin, and His righteousness would justify salvation to the uttermost.

The Bible was given by the Spirit for this life; and Christ was made flesh for this world, and His resurrection from the dead was to teach us in this world of the future life and of the relation of the present to the future.

The Spirit comes to this world to convict of sin and of righteousness and of judgment, none of which were necessary at such a sacrifice, except as affecting probation in this life.

After death comes immediately the individual judgment, when believers are received by Christ to Himself; and at the end of the world, when the probation of the race is ended, comes the general judgment, which is not so much a judgment as an exhibition of the justice of God in saving sinners through the sacrifice of Christ, and the grand triumphal jubilee of redemption, which concerns not so much the judgment of man as the eternal glory of God.

Then certainly all things concerning the Spirit's work in redemption are ended forever, and the kingdom of Christ is fully come. Hereafter there is no more probation of the Spirit, or redemption by Christ—the books are sealed forever.

There is also to be considered another fact: that more time, without the Spirit's work, would be of no avail whatsoever in making choice. Any longer probation would mean more sin, and growth in sin; and indefinite probation, indefinite sinning. The tendency of sin is to permanency; it grows worse and worse with time, and the conscience hardens. The sinner under a limited probation, if uncertain, loses feeling, and easily becomes thoughtless, and even a blasphemer. Liberty becomes license, and license recklessness. First ungodly, then a sinner, and then an enemy of God is the order of sin's progression.

The shorter the limit of life the less will there be of sin; and the shorter the limit of probation the greater the probability of repentance. When men lived nearly a thousand years they became very great sinners, and God had to destroy them from the face of the earth with a flood. It was then said, "My Spirit shall not always strive with man." Life was shortened after the flood for the greater salvation of the race.

The sinner goes into the other life with the same carnal heart, with its sinful momentum of years, to be under the same holy law; and if there should be any further probation under the same conditions, with no other grace of Christ or influence of the Spirit, there would be no more hope of change. He would grow worse instead of better under unlimited probation. What more or better could the Spirit do or offer in another life than He has already done here?

Our Saviour taught that between Lazarus and Dives there was a "great gulf fixed, so that they that would pass from one to the other could not," and that if they on earth would not hear Moses and the prophets, they would not hear though one rose from the dead.

"Who resist the blood-stained cross,
Resist the uttermost that heaven can do."

The whole plan and history of redemption; all the invitations and warnings and promises of the Gospel, so urgent and fearful and blessed, are predicted on a present probation.

We are exhorted, "Quench not the Spirit,"

and "Grieve not the Spirit of God whereby ye are sealed unto the day of redemption." That by which we are acknowledged and confirmed as Christ's in the day of redemption is the seal of the Spirit, and where He is grieved there is no seal.

The Jews were guilty of resisting the Holy Spirit, and were exhorted, "To-day if ye will hear His voice harden not your hearts," as those to whom He sware in His wrath they should not enter into His rest; and much more is this true of this "day of salvation" in which is our probation.

When holy love such as that the Spirit shows to sinners becomes holy wrath, in view of their sins and impenitence and unbelief, it is as fearful as the love was blessed. Divine justice is no fiction, and the wrath of the Lamb must be unendurable.

There is an awful majesty in these words from the Epistle to the Hebrews, "He that despised Moses' law died without mercy under two or three witnesses; of how much sorer punishment, suppose ye, shall he be thought worthy, who hath trodden under foot the Son of God, and hath counted the blood of the covenant wherewith he was sanctified an unholy thing, and hath done despite to the Spirit of grace? For we know Him that saith, Vengeance is mine; I will recompense, saith the Lord." " It is a fearful thing to fall into the hands of the living God."

The terrible punishment visited upon Ananias and Sapphira was intended to be an example of the Holy Spirit's wrath against those who would deceive Him and abuse His mercy.

The Spirit comes in the name of the Father and the Son, and will resent any affront put on them, as they will any sin against Him. His work is the last effort of the long-suffering of Divine love to save the sinner; and when He is driven away grieved, there is nothing more that can be done for his salvation. Divine love is exhausted. His condemnation is as certain as if he were already dead, and had passed the ordeal of judgment. He is already and always condemned who does not believe in Christ; not to add the sin against the Holy Spirit.

It may not be in itself a worse sin than others; it may be a seemingly small offense which finally grieves the Spirit to depart forever. Persistent unbelief will quench His strivings until He leaves, nevermore to return, after which the door of hope is shut.

While blasphemy against the Holy Spirit "hath never forgiveness," and is an "eternal sin," the final act of unbelief has the same effect, and is also an eternal sin.

Probation is of the Spirit in any case, and

when He finally leaves the sinner there is no more offer of grace, no opportunity for repentance and renewal. Hope dies forever. The sinner has died the second death; closed his probation by his own act, and banished himself from God and heaven forever.

Vengeance is rendered " to them that know not God and to them that obey not the Gospel of our Lord Jesus Christ: who shall suffer punishment, even eternal destruction from the face of the Lord and the glory of His might, when He shall come to be glorified in His saints, and to be marvelled at in all them that believe, in that day."

Unbelief shuts the gate of heaven. It is no fiction of Dante's which writes over the gate of hell,

" All hope abandon, ye who enter here."

CHAPTER XII.

THE COMMUNION OF THE HOLY SPIRIT.

THE Apostle Paul had a beautiful custom, in common with all the world, of gathering up at the close of his epistles all good wishes in one prayer of valediction.

At the close of the second epistle to the Corinthians he reaches the climax of blessing in what is called, because of its supreme excellence, the Apostolic benediction—" The grace of our Lord Jesus Christ and the love of God and the communion of the Holy Ghost be with you all." This is the trinity of divine blessing in the planning and procuring and communication of redemption; originating in the love of the Father, purchased by the grace of Christ, and received through the fellowship of the Spirit. This blessing finds its culmination in the " communion of the Holy Ghost," the channel through which it reaches us, so that, in the final analysis of redemption, the vital link is the work of the Spirit, without which the love of the Father and the grace of Christ would be fruitless. And the word

THE COMMUNION OF THE HOLY SPIRIT. 165

"Communion" expresses the fullness of the blessedness of the relation of the Spirit to us, or rather of our mutual relationship. The apostle prays that we may have all things in common with the Holy Spirit; so that there may be between us and Him an unbroken intercourse, a mutual giving and receiving, a friendly conversation and fellowship.

We find at the outset a difficulty in understanding how there can be such communion between man and the Spirit of God. "God is a Spirit, and they that worship Him must worship Him in spirit and in truth." Man is more than spirit,—"spirit, soul, and body"—and herein lies the difficulty in understanding how the Spirit of God, unseen and unheard, can come into communion with him. This is made plain when we consider that man is also a spirit and has all the attributes and qualities of spirit; and that his spirit is the highest part of man, which should rule his mind and body for spiritual service. His spirit is his very person, that which is the ruling and responsible part, and in which he is in the image of God. His spirit manifests itself in consciousness, intelligence, choice, will, affections, and moral feelings, and through these powers he holds communion with his fellow-men, and in the same way also with the Spirit of God—with this difference, however, that the Spirit of God comes into direct and immediate and personal contact with man's spirit in his very consciousness, where they can commune face to face, eye to eye, thought to thought, feeling to feeling, will to will, heart to heart, the spirit of man transparent to the Holy Spirit; who is able to come into the inner sanctuary of his conscious being, so that his body becomes the temple of the Holy Spirit, and he can thus glorify God in his body and his spirit, which are God's.

This access of spirit to spirit gives scope for worship, which must, of course, be sincere to be acceptable, since the Holy Spirit knows immediately what is in man. In worship man expresses the true and natural relation between himself and his Creator. Man is a religious or worshipping being, and is not satisfied until he finds God. Spiritual worship will be the outgoing of intelligence, emotion, affection, choice, will, and conscience to God in answer to the corresponding relations in him. Knowledge, love, and service will be given to God. Worship finds expression in prayer and devotion, but its culmination and perfection are in the communion of the Holy Spirit, which is a conscious, abiding fellowship of the spirit of man with the Spirit of God, in the fulfillment of every spiritual relation; the perfect harmony and intercourse of spiritual environment.

The law of spiritual life which shall produce

such worship would subordinate the body and the desires of this world to the spirit's life, and submit and devote everything to God.

And while this demands self-denial and sacrifice, and even the death of all below, and finally death to the world itself, it is the law of the spirit's highest life, and brings it to the fruition of the glory of God. Willing obedience to this law implies a state of spiritual-mindedness, which sets the choice and current of being, the supreme love of the human spirit on God, which is the condition of the Holy Spirit's indwelling and communion.

But, right here, we are met with the fact that man is not obedient to the law of his spirit, and will not have the communion of the Holy Spirit, however important and precious this privilege may be. He is carnal, and is not subject to the law of God, and will not be; and there is nothing in him in which the Spirit can take delight.

The Spirit is the Holy Spirit, holy in being and character, in all His attributes and perfections and words and works; in thought and desire and feeling; in person and manifestation and companionship, and man is under the government of His holy power according to His holy law. In His sight sin is exceeding sinful even unto death, to be banished forever from His presence and the glory of His power.

Now appears the love of God to man passing knowledge, as revealed in the wondrous plan of redemption. The Father in His divine compassion saw His once upright creature, made in His image, fallen, ruined, and lost; and asked for one to take his place and bear his guilt and make atonement; when the Son of God, in pity, offered Himself as man's Redeemer; and the Father in His great love gave Him up and sent Him into the world to save sinners; while the Holy Spirit also sanctioned this plan of redemption, and on His part offered His power and presence to make effectual the sacrifice of Christ in its application to man's salvation. Thus the love of the Father planned, the love of the Son purchased, and the love of the Spirit completed the redemption of man. The Lord Jesus Christ became incarnate, was obedient unto death, even the death of the cross; paid the price, rose from the dead, and ascended up to the right hand of God, having purchased the privilege of an everlasting Intercessor, until the kingdoms of this world should become His, according to the promise of the Father.

Thus He fulfilled the conditions upon which He could proclaim the covenant of grace to sinners, and freely invite all to come to Him and be saved.

The grace of our Lord Jesus Christ is the

supreme blessing of His love. While He was with His disciples in the world, they thought themselves divinely favored, and that nothing could be better for them than His presence; but He tells them that it would be better for them if He should go away that He might send another Comforter unto them, who should abide with them forever. This Comforter the Father and Himself would give unto them without measure, and He would reveal and apply the things of Christ, glorifying Him, convincing the world of sin and of righteousness and of judgment.

Pentecost witnessed the power and glory of the Spirit's coming; as He was poured out like a rushing wind and like a flaming fire, when He began to establish the Church of Christ in its new testament; and the whole record of the Acts of the Apostles is His account of His own acts as He taught and filled the Apostles, and worked through them, showing how He would work in and with and for the Church in all time.

And we now live under the administration of the Holy Spirit, which is even more glorious than that of the law and of Christ in person. He is fitted to be the Divine Executive, who knows the mind of God, and also as a Spirit knows immediately the mind of man, and can reveal and teach the things of God, illuminating, convicting, and working with all power, and grace, and truth.

As the executive of the holy law the Spirit has no other alternative for the sinner than obedience or death. But Christ was the end of the law for righteousness to every one that believeth. All who believe in Him are saved from the curse of the law of sin and death. Yet He is forced to exclaim, "Ye will not come to me that ye might have life." The carnal heart will not change itself, and cannot, and no one of himself will ever come to Him. The death of Christ, which provided an all-sufficient sacrifice for sin, and purchased full and free redemption, would avail nothing, unless some one shall lead the sinner to accept its benefits. All that is expressed in His cross were lost to mankind, great as was the love of the Father and the Son, had not the Spirit come to make it effectual. But for the sacrifice of Christ, the Holy Spirit could have nothing to do with man, and it is only in Christ's name that He undertakes his salvation. All things done by the Spirit in His administration are in the name of Christ. In His own great love He comes even into a sinner's heart to cleanse and change and sanctify it until it shall, through the grace of Christ, be fitted for glory. Thus we have the origin and ground and privilege of the communion of the Holy Spirit. He would take of the things of Christ, and shew them unto us for His glory and our glorification.

At first the friendship is all on one side, and His coming is uninvited and unwelcome; and we shut our ears to His message and our hearts to His love. He comes in faithful love to discover to us our sin and to convict us of its guilt; a most unpleasant work for Him, but necessary for us, that we may see our lost condition and our need of the grace and intercession of Christ. He convicts of sin that He may persuade us to trust in the righteousness of Christ. When we do this He speaks pardon and peace, and sheds abroad the love of Christ in our hearts, and gives us the joy of adoption; bearing witness that we are the children of God. Until then we knew not the love of Christ and had no joy in the Holy Ghost, and cared not for His communion.

Now begins a fellowship that shall become nearer and dearer as time goes on. Having renewed our hearts by His power and grace, He takes personal delight in us and will not cease His friendship till He presents us to the Father, in the name of Christ, complete and glorified. He makes our bodies the place of His indwelling, and we give Him a sanctuary in our hearts. The things which the eye hath not seen, nor the ear heard, nor have entered into the mind of the carnal man, He shows unto us. Having begun in us a good work, He will, as our Sanctifier, continue it until the day of Jesus Christ. He becomes our Teacher and leads us into all truth, calling it to remembrance, illuminating with His light, strengthening in temptation and trial, upholding and comforting in all afflictions, helping our infirmities, making all things work together for our good, that He may make Christ unto us wisdom and righteousness and sanctification and redemption.

Having this communion, we "pray in the Spirit," and He also prays with us that we may seek the fullness of the blessing of the intercession of Christ for us; and when we know not what to pray for as we ought, He maketh intercession for us with groanings which cannot be uttered. Through prayer He brings us to God face to face, and calls out our minds and wills and affections Godward; especially does He reveal sin and keep from sin, and help to overcome easily besetting sins, and bestow all grace to help in every time of need. As He communes with us thus, we are brought more and more into sympathy with Him in glorifying the love of Christ, and in efforts to spread abroad His kingdom. And He would train us for usefulness and honor in His service. He would work all spiritual graces in us, that He might also bestow all spiritual gifts upon us and use us in all good works. The more He reveals to us the love of Christ the more do we pray and labor for the coming of His kingdom and the doing of His will. We give ourselves joyfully to the work of His Church and enter heartily into her most blessed mission of giving the Gospel to every creature.

Every spiritual blessing depends on the communion of the Holy Spirit. But for Him we never would have known the sinfulness of sin, never have sought the grace of Christ, never have been born into spiritual life, never have become sons of God, never have persevered in a Christian life, never have lived lives of prayer, never have become workers together with Christ, never have been able to rejoice in the hope of the glory of God. And it will be only as we keep our minds on the things of the Spirit that we shall attain to the fullness of life and to abiding peace. We must be *kept* by the Spirit, and our sanctification will not be completed so long as we are in the flesh.

We shall need His teaching and help and comfort continually.

Daily shall we need grace and deliverance from evil. Our discipline in righteousness is not yet ended. Sufferings and afflictions, like those of the Master, are before us. There will be many a contest with sin before we lay hold on eternal life. Not for a moment may we undertake to live without the help of the Spirit in our infirmities. And there are graces in which we are to grow; with which He would ornament our characters, which we would have Him work in us, adding grace to grace. There are deep mines of precious truth yet undiscovered or unused, bonanzas of spiritual riches awaiting us, and heavenly treasures inexhaustible, which may be laid up in store. There are heights of spiritual knowledge stretching out before us from which we may catch visions of heavenly glory. We have not yet known all the sinfulness of sin, nor all the righteousness of Christ. The love of Christ, which has heights and depths and length and breadth passing knowledge, is yet to be shed abroad in our hearts until we are filled with the fullness of God. With this knowledge of Christ we see the prince of this world judged; and that nothing in this world, and no power of evil, can separate us from the love of God which is in Jesus Christ our Lord; and this begets within us a peace, a confidence, an assurance, full and abiding, of a faith which rejoices and triumphs in victory through Christ, giving thanks as if it were already ours, counting even death a release to our heavenly home.

With such communion of the Spirit we shall not enter heaven as strangers, for our citizenship is there already; but we shall be at home there, having our joys, our loves, our hopes, our friends,

THE COMMUNION OF THE HOLY SPIRIT. 175

our hearts already there. Along with this communion of the Holy Spirit goes the communion of saints, the fellowship of friend with friend, bound together by a common love for Christ, having their faith and joy and hope in common, and often sitting together in heavenly places in Christ Jesus; a fellowship that shall abide with the communion of the Spirit, to become nearer and dearer through the clearer revelation and perfect sight of heavenly vision, face to face.

It is evident from what we have seen of the love of the Spirit that nothing on His part will break or alloy this blessed communion, founded in the love of the Father and the grace of Christ. If we fail of it in any measure it will be the fault of our own sin and unbelief and unfaithfulness. If we banish Him from our thoughts and keep not our minds on the things of the Spirit; if we turn His temple into a house of merchandise, or devote it to pleasure and worldliness instead of prayer; if we defile it with sin; if we give place to the evil one and allow him to fill our hearts; if we neglect or cease to trust in and love Christ; if we leave our Bibles unread, and our closets unopened, and cease to frequent the house of God, and the place of prayer, and to engage in the work of the Lord, then He must withdraw from us and withhold His grace and leave us to ourselves, until we learn by a sad experience our ignorance and weakness and folly, and do again the first works. Not to open our hearts to Him, not to give Him a welcome and an abiding-place, to grieve Him, to provoke Him, to quench Him, is ingratitude and unbelief, most dangerous and most sinful; for should He finally depart, the love of the Father and the grace of the Lord Jesus Christ were all vain to us, and the door of hope is shut and heavenly fellowship is impossible evermore.

To know Him and to be known of Him is to know and be known of God and Jesus Christ, whom He has sent, which is eternal life. To see Him and be seen of Him is to see heaven and have heaven begun in us; to love Him and to be loved of Him is to have the love of the Father and the Son perfected in us.

To be filled with the Holy Spirit is to be filled with all the fullness of God; and to be taught of Him is to have heaven opened, and to see Jesus Christ sitting on the right hand of God. To have His communion is to have Jesus Christ Himself abiding with us through a Comforter, who is better than His earthly presence. Communing with the Holy Spirit, we have forgiveness of sins, justification, adoption, and sanctification; peace, joy, and hope of glory; light in darkness, strength in weakness, and comfort in affliction. At times even here we know not whether we are in the body or out of the body, so does He fill us with His glory, taking us up into the third heaven of delight. Then again we are with Christ on the mount of transfiguration, ravished with His presence and His love. Waiting in this tabernacle, we groan, being burdened, looking not at the things which are seen, but at the things which are unseen and eternal, longing until mortality shall be swallowed up of life.

If the communion of the Holy Spirit and the communion of saints be such sweet and blessed fellowship here below, what shall be their fruition in the clear sight of heavenly glory?

Having all things in common with the Holy Spirit, the good of earth is ours and heaven is ours, the Father is ours and Christ is ours; all things are ours of life and life eternal.

We gather up all blessings and put all prayers in one when we pray : " The communion of the Holy Spirit be with you all."

www.ingramcontent.com/pod-product-compliance
Lightning Source LLC
Chambersburg PA
CBHW032142160426
43197CB00008B/749